Childcraft

T H E   H O W   A N D   W H Y   L I B R A R Y

VOLUME 11

Make and Do

World Book, Inc.

a Scott Fetzer company

Chicago   London   Sydney   Toronto

Childcraft—The How and Why Library
(Reg. U.S. Pat. and T.M. Off. —Marca Registrada)
© 1996 World Book, Inc. All rights reserved. This
volume may not be reproduced in whole or in part in any
form without prior written permission from the publisher.

World Book, Inc.
525 W. Monroe
Chicago, IL 60661

© 1995, 1994, 1993, 1991, 1990, 1989, 1987, 1986, 1985 by World Book,
Inc. © 1982, 1981, 1980, 1979 U.S.A. by World Book-Childcraft
International, Inc. © 1976, 1974, 1973, 1971, 1970, 1969, 1968, 1965,
1964 U.S.A. by Field Enterprises Educational Corporation.
International Copyright © 1987, 1986, 1985 by World Book, Inc.
International Copyright © 1982, 1981, 1980, 1979 by World Book-
Childcraft International, Inc.
International Copyright © 1976, 1974, 1973, 1971, 1970, 1969, 1968,
1965, 1964 by Field Enterprises Educational Corporation.

ISBN 0-7166-0196-6
Library of Congress Catalog Card Number 95-61673
Printed in the United States of America
1 2 3 4 5 6 7 8 9 10 99 98 97 96

Make and Do and You

An adventure is an exciting happening! And that's what
Make and Do is all about—an adventure into the world of arts
and crafts, a world in which *you* can make exciting things
happen.

Here, you'll find all kinds of wonderful things to make and
do. There are easy projects to start with and more difficult
ones to make once you've had some practice. And there are
projects you can make with your mom and dad or a grown-up
friend.

Most of the sections in this book begin with a few pages
of "Helpful hints." There you'll find out about the basic skills
or materials you will need to make the projects in the section.
If you haven't mastered the special skills needed, here's
a chance to learn them.

Before you begin a project, read *all* of the directions and
gather all of the materials you will need. Try to picture
what you have to do in each step. Then follow the easy,
step-by-step directions.

Be careful with all tools, especially sharp or pointed ones.
When the directions tell you to ask for help, don't be afraid
to ask a grown-up to give you a hand.

Many of the sections end with two pages of "more ideas"—
where you are on your own. If you have made most of the
projects in the section, you'll find it fun to make some of these
other projects. And the more you make and do, the more
ideas you will think of for projects of your own.

So, look through this book and see all of the adventures
that are waiting for you!

Volume 11

Make and Do

Contents

Toys, Crafts, and Make-Believe

Let's begin with a craft box!

A craft box is like a magic box. You put in a lot of junk and ordinary things. Then you add the magic ingredients—a little glue, some paint, a piece of string, your imagination. And out comes a happy surprise—toys, crafts, and make-believe!

Start with a big box. If you still have it, the carton your *Childcraft* books came in would make a good craft box. But an even bigger box is better. Then start filling the box with all the things you'll want to use to make and do.

Fill your craft box

Where can you find the things to fill your craft box? Why, all around you! But before you take anything, be sure to ask if you may have it.

Start your make-and-do collecting adventure at home. You'll find lots of things in the attic, in closets, in the kitchen, and in the garage.

Of course, you'll have to buy some things, such as paints and brushes, at a local craft store. But there are many free things outdoors.

You'll find nuts, sticks, and leaves in the woods. You can get sand and shells at the beach. And you'll find stones and flowers in your yard. You will be surprised by what you can find if you keep your eyes open.

Now that you know *where* to look for things to fill your craft box, here are some of the things to look for.

Things to save

balloons
bottle caps
bricks
buttons
cardboard boxes and tubes
cloth scraps (burlap, felt, etc.)
coat hangers
combs
corks
drinking straws
egg cartons
flowers
food trays and baskets
hairpins
ice-cream sticks
jar lids
keys
leaves
milk cartons
nails
newspapers and magazines
paper, colored and plain
paper bags
paper clips
paper napkins and towels
paper plates and cups
picture frames
pins and needles
pipe cleaners
plastic bottles and jars
pocket mirrors
rubber bands

sand
screws
sea shells
seeds of all kinds
shirt cardboards
socks and stockings
spools
spoons and forks
sticks
stones and pebbles
string
thread
tin cans
tissue paper
toothpicks
used gift wrapping and ribbon
washers
yarn

Things to buy

colored chalk
construction paper
crayons
crepe paper
felt-tip pens
paints and paintbrushes
ruler
scissors
transparent tape
white glue

Your first project

For your first project, try decorating your craft
box. You can paint it or cover it with colorful
paper. Then splash it with paint or glue on
designs of felt or paper. It's your craft box,
so you decide how you'd like it to look.

Rhythm-band parade

These musical instruments are easy to make. When you've made them all, you and your friends can have a rhythm-band parade.

Cymbals

Crash, crash, crash go the big brass cymbals. Use two pot lids for cymbals.

Drum

Boom, boom, boom goes the big bass drum. For your drum, decorate an oatmeal box or a coffee can with a plastic lid. Ask a grown-up to punch two holes near the top of the can or box. Thread string through the holes and tie the ends together. Hang the drum around your neck. Use a spoon for a drumstick.

Sandpaper Scratchers

Sh, sh, sh say the sandpaper scratchers. Use thumbtacks or staples to fasten sandpaper to two blocks of wood. Rub the blocks together.

Hummer Kazoo

Buzz, buzz, buzz a merry tune with this hum, hum, hummer kazoo. Fold a piece of wax paper over a comb. Press the wax paper and comb against your lips and hum a song.

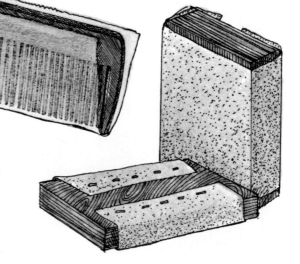

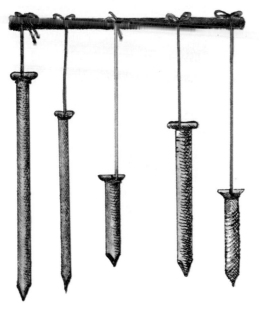

Chimes

Tinkle, tinkle, clink is the jingle of
these chimes. Tie nails to a stick and
hit them with a spoon.

Finger Cymbals

Ching, ching, ching ring these little finger cymbals. Ask a grown-up to use a hammer and nail to punch holes in two bottle caps or lids. Tie little loops of yarn or string in the holes to hold the cymbals on your fingers. Hit the cymbals together.

Banjo Box

Plink, plink, plink on this bright banjo box. Cut a hole in the top of a box. Then tape the top to the box. Stretch rubber bands around the box and over the hole, and you're ready to go! Try rubber bands of different sizes and thicknesses. Listen to what happens.

Flute

Toot, toot, toot on this merry little flute. Use the point of a pencil to poke holes in one side of a cardboard tube. Cover one end of the tube with wax paper. Hold the wax paper in place with a rubber band. Hum into the uncovered end of the tube as you move your fingers over the holes.

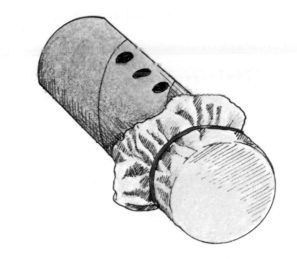

Tambourine

Shake-a-shake-a-shake these tambourine plates. Decorate two pie tins or paper plates. Put some seeds in one plate. Put the other plate face down on top of the first plate. Staple or tape the plates together. Or, punch holes around the rim of the plates and sew them together with yarn. Add some paper or ribbon streamers.

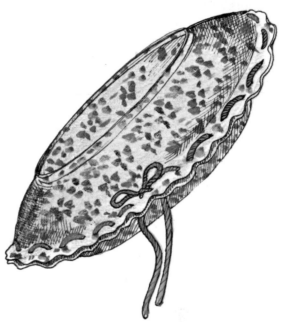

Maracas

Rattle, rattle, rattle these maracas to the beat of the music. Ask a grown-up to use a hammer and nail to punch a hole in the bottom of an empty soda-pop can. Push an unsharpened pencil through the hole in the bottom of the can and out through the drinking hole in the top. Then push the end of the pencil into the narrow part of the drinking hole. Put a handful of seeds into the can. Put tape over the hole and decorate the can.

Strings and things

You can use string to make other things. Or, you can use other things to make a string. Here's how.

Macaroni Jewelry

Dip large macaroni into different food colors for a few seconds. Lay the macaroni on paper towels until it dries. Cut a piece of yarn long enough to make a necklace or bracelet. Wrap it at one end with transparent tape. Tie a piece of macaroni at the other end. String the macaroni. Then untie the piece of macaroni and tie the yarn ends together.

String-a-Ling Telephone

Say "Hi" to your friends on this telephone made from string and two paper cups. Punch a small hole in the bottom of each paper cup. Thread a long string through the holes. Tie a button to each end of the string. You take one cup and have your friend take the other. Stretch out the string and talk into the cups. Take turns talking and listening.

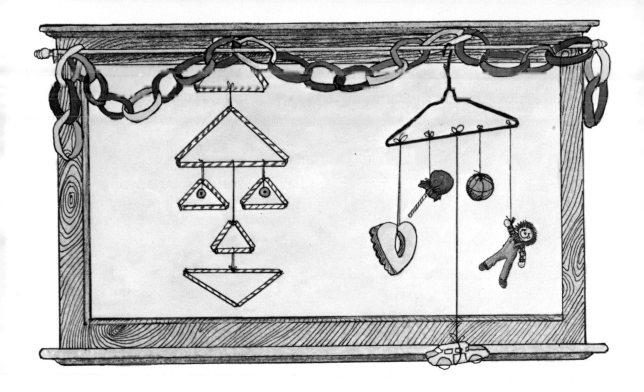

Paper Chains

Make colorful paper chains with strips of construction paper and tape or glue. If you want, you can decorate the strips before you make the chain. Hang the chain from the ceiling or string it around your Christmas tree.

Gadget Mobile

Use a string to hang gadgets on a coat hanger. You can use cookie cutters, paper clips, old combs, buttons, macaroni, or anything else you find.

String-a-Straw Mobile

You can make many interesting mobiles and ornaments out of paper or plastic drinking straws. Cut the straws at different angles and lengths. Use a needle and heavy button thread to string the straws together. Begin by tying three straws in a triangle. Then tie other straws to the triangle.

Let's pretend

It's fun to make believe you're someone else. When you pretend, you can be anyone you want to be and do anything you want to do.

Doctor For a stethoscope, tape a long loop of yarn to a spool. Hang the stethoscope around your neck.

Police Officer or **Sheriff** Cut out a cardboard star. Cover the star with foil. Pin the star on your shirt.

King or **Queen** To make a crown, use a strip of cardboard long enough to go around your head. Cut points along one edge of the strip. Bend the strip into a circle and tape the ends together. Cover the crown with foil. Glue on construction paper jewels. Use a big scarf for a cape.

Explorer Glue two toilet-paper tubes together to make binoculars.

Cowboy Tie a kerchief around your neck. Use a piece of rope for a lasso. A broom with a paper-bag horse's head makes a fine horse. Tie a piece of string around the horse's head and use the ends for reins.

Hula Dancer Cut off the bottom of a large paper bag. Draw a line about 3 inches (8 cm) from the top of the bag. Make long strips by cutting up to the line. Tape paper shoulder straps to the skirt band. Glue crumpled tissue paper to the shoulder straps for flowers.

World Traveler Get some old magazines and cut out pictures of the places you'd like to visit. Use a shopping bag for a suitcase. Line up chairs to make a train or plane. Hop on board and you're off to faraway places and exciting adventures.

Camper or **Bandit** Make a tent. Tie a piece of rope between the backs of two chairs. Put a blanket or sheet over the rope. Hold the ends of the blanket down with some heavy books. Or, make a hideout. Put a blanket or a sheet over a table.

Airplane Pilot Draw an outline of the instrument panel on a large cardboard box. Glue on spools, jar lids, bottle caps, and mirrors for the instruments. Cut a control wheel, out of cardboard. Poke a pencil through the center of the wheel. Wind rubber bands around the pencil, above and below the wheel to hold it in place. Poke the pencil through the instrument panel. Use rubber bands to hold the pencil in place.

Wild Animal Make a mask out of a large grocery bag. Glue on ears made of construction paper. Use crayons to draw the eyes, nose, and mouth. Cut out eye holes so you can see where you are going.

Let's build

Rocket Ship

Use plastic containers or tin cans of all sizes. Glue or tape the cans together, with the biggest can on the bottom. If you have an old funnel, tape it to the top can. Paint the cans to look like a rocket ship, and you're ready to blast off to the moon.

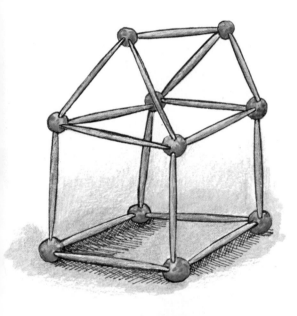

Toothpick and Pea Constructions

Soak dried peas in water for about eight hours, or use canned peas. Then stick toothpicks into the peas. You can build amazing constructions. Set the constructions aside until the peas dry. As the peas dry, they will shrink and make your constructions sturdy.

Milk-Carton Blocks

You can make a fine set of building blocks with small milk cartons. Cut open the flaps and tape them down. If you paste paper on the cartons, you'll be able to paint and decorate them.

Card Houses

Use a deck of playing cards to build a house or a pyramid. It can be done, but you must be patient and very careful when you build with cards.

Box Structures

Glue boxes in a stack and paint them to look like a totem pole. If you have very large cartons, make a house. Cut out doors and windows. Then glue the cartons together so you can crawl from one carton to another.

More toys!

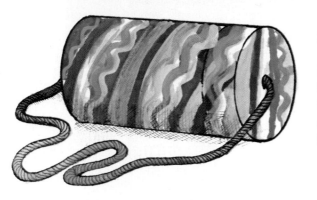

Shoebox Train

Pull your toys in a shoebox choo-choo train. Paint the boxes to look like train cars. Then punch a hole in the ends of each box. Tie the boxes together with string and buttons.

Toddler Pull-Toy

Help a toddler make this fun toy. Punch a hole in the top and bottom of an empty round box. Thread a long piece of yarn or string through the holes and tie the ends together. Put a handful of seeds in the box. Tape the top to the box. Decorate the box.

Tops

Tops are easy to make. And they're good toys, both indoors and out. You can make all kinds of tops with spools, jar lids, or any other round object in which you can punch a hole. Or, cut out a circle from stiff cardboard and poke a hole in the center. Push a stick, pencil, or nail through the hole. To hold the stick in place, wind rubber bands around it above and below the cardboard.

Twirlers

A twirler will give you a surprise when you color it and watch it twirl. Use a compass, a can top, or a pencil and a string to draw a 4-inch (10-cm) circle on stiff cardboard. Cut out the circle and color it, as shown. Punch two holes in the circle, each about $\frac{3}{8}$ inch (9 mm) from the center of the circle. Thread about 2 feet (60 cm) of string through the holes and tie the ends together. Twist the string and then stretch it out to make the twirler spin.

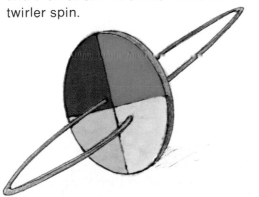

Tin-Can Stilts

Walk tall on these tin-can stilts. Start with two large coffee cans. Ask a grown-up to use a hammer and nail to punch two holes near the unopened end of each can. Thread plastic clothesline through the holes and tie the ends together. Pull up on the strings with your hands as you walk on your tin-can stilts.

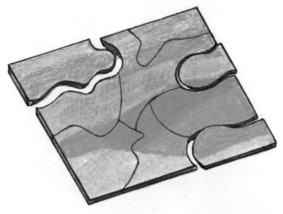

Parachute Pilot

Toss this parachute into the air and watch the pilot float to the ground. Cut four pieces of thin string, each about 12 inches (30 cm) long. Tie the strings to the corners of a large handkerchief. Then tie all four strings together. For the pilot, tie a wooden spool or clothespin to the string. Fold the corners of the parachute into the middle. Then roll it up and toss it into the air.

Picture Puzzles

Glue a magazine picture or a map on a piece of thin cardboard. Cut the picture into puzzle pieces. If you're using a map, cut along the state or province lines. Now try to put the puzzle together.

Catch-Can

Catch-Can is a skill game you can play by yourself. Ask a grown-up to use a hammer and nail to punch a hole in the bottom of a small vegetable or soup can. Thread about 12 inches (30 cm) of string through the hole. Tie a heavy button to each end of the string. Let the string hang down outside the can. Hold the can in your hand. Now swing the string and try to catch the button in the can.

Flying Saucers

Play flying-saucer catch with a friend.
To make your own flying saucers,
decorate plastic coffee-can lids.

Gadget Friends

You can put on a puppet show with
these gadget friends. Old toothbrushes,
whisk brooms, wooden spoons, work
gloves, corks, sponges, feather
dusters, and scouring pads are good
things to use. To turn the gadgets into
friends, decorate them with paint and
bits of string, yarn, and cloth.

Cars and Trucks

You can use shoeboxes and milk
cartons to make cars and trucks that
roll. Use pencils for the axles. Tape
them to the bottom of a box. Cut out
circles from stiff cardboard for the
wheels. Poke holes in the center of
the circles. Wind rubber bands
around the axles, put on the wheels,
and wind on more rubber bands to
hold the wheels in place. To make
your cars look like trucks, fire engines,
or ambulances, glue on other boxes
and decorate them.

Crazy creatures

Paper-Bag Puppets

All of these puppets started as plain paper bags. Draw or paint faces and bodies on the bags. If you want, tape or glue on construction paper and yarn decorations. Poke holes in the sides of the bag for your fingers, stuff the head with crumpled paper, and tie a string around the neck. Or, cup your fingers in the bag to make the head move.

Paper-Bag Pets

Paper bags make fat, friendly creatures. To make these pets, you'll need at least two paper bags that are the same size. Stuff one bag with crumpled newspaper. Pull the other bag over the stuffed one. Tape the bags together. If you want, use smaller bags to make a head and feet. Stuff these bags and glue them to the body bag. Turn the bags into pets with crayons, paint, construction paper, yarn, and glue. Or, to make a marionette, use string to tie the pet to a long stick.

Egg-Carton Animals

Here's a zooful of animals you can make from egg cartons. To start, cut apart all the little cups that make the carton. Then cut the cups to form legs, ears, wings, fish scales, and animal tails. Glue the cups together in the shapes of animals. You can use toilet paper tubes for some of the bodies. Then paint the animals. If you use Styrofoam egg cartons, mix some laundry detergent into your tempera paints. Add construction paper, pipe cleaner, and yarn decorations.

Milk-Carton Menagerie

It's easy to see these strange little creatures began life as ordinary milk cartons. You can use milk cartons of all sizes, but the small cartons you get in school and the pint sized cartons used for cream seem to work best. All you have to do is paint the cartons and add construction paper, drinking straw, and yarn decorations. Mix some laundry detergent into your tempera paints so the paint will stick to the wax-coated carton. The pets in the picture will help you get started.

Things that move

Motorboat

Motorboats are fun to play with in a
pool or tub. Close and glue the spout
on a half-gallon milk carton. Cut out
the spout side of the carton for the
top of the boat. Poke a hole in the
bottom of the boat, near the back. Put
a balloon in the boat and push the
balloon's neck through the hole. Blow
up the balloon. Hold the neck closed
with your fingers. Put the boat in the
water and let go. Watch the boat putt,
putt, putt away.

Oriental Paper-Bag Kite

An Oriental paper-bag kite will fly
tied to a tree or will follow you as
you run along. Cut out a circle from
stiff cardboard. Cut out the center of
the circle to make a ring. Tape the
cut in the ring. Tie three short pieces
of string to the ring. Then tie the strings
together. Trace the inside of the ring
on the bottom of a paper bag. Cut out
the hole. Glue the ring inside the bag,
with the strings coming out of the
hole. Decorate the bag and attach a
long kite string.

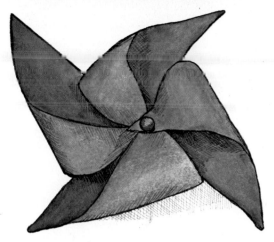

Pinwheel

Start with a square piece of construction paper. Draw an X, from corner to corner. Cut from each corner halfway to the center. Fold over every other point and tape or staple these points at the center. Push a thumbtack through the center and into the eraser on a pencil. Blow on the pinwheel or run with it and watch it spin.

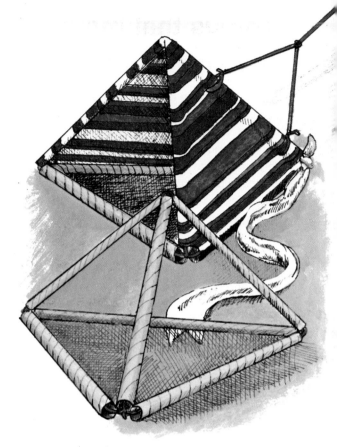

Drinking-Straw Kite

Here's a high-flying kite you can play with in the city or the country. String six straws together to make a four-sided shape called a tetrahedron. It's easiest if you suck the string through the straws.

Cover two sides with one piece of tissue paper. Use the tetrahedron to measure the paper. Cut the paper about 1 inch (2.5 cm) larger than the sides. Glue the paper around the straws.

Attach the two bridle strings exactly as shown. About one-third of the way from the top front edge of the kite, poke small holes in the paper. Then thread a string through the holes and around the straw. Tie the string to the straw. Then attach a slightly longer string near the bottom front edge. Tie the two bridle strings together. Then tie light kite string to the bridle strings.

To make a tail, cut several strips of tissue paper about 2 inches (5 cm) wide and 3 feet (1 m) long. Tie the tail to the bottom front edge of the kite. Then run and watch your kite follow you as it goes up, up, and away. If your kite doesn't fly well, adjust the bridle strings.

Carnival games

Egg-Carton Bean Race

Start with an egg carton. Write a
number, from one to six, in each cup
on one side of the egg carton.
Write the numbers in order or mix
them up. Write the same numbers in
the cups on the other side. Each
player picks up beans by sucking
through a straw. Use big beans, such
as lima beans, that won't go through the
straw. The number of beans put into
each cup must match the number in the
cup. The player who finishes first wins.

Tiddlywinks

Use a tuna or cat-food can for the cup.
Use flat buttons for the playing
pieces. Paint each group of four
buttons a different color. Each player
gets four buttons plus a larger button
to use as a flipper.

Draw a circle on the ground. Put the
can in the center of the circle. Place
the pieces at the edge of the circle.
Try to flip the pieces into the can.
If you miss the can, you must flip the
piece from where it lands. The first
one to flip all his pieces into the
can wins.

Tin-Can Bowling

Arrange ten tin cans in the form of
a triangle. Stand about 6 feet (2 m)
away and roll a ball at the cans. See
how many cans you can knock down.

Sailboat Race

First, color and cut out a paper sail. You can write your name or a number on the sail. Poke a toothpick through the sail. Then, put a little lump of Plasticine modeling clay in a bottle cap or jar lid. Push the toothpick into the clay. Fill the kitchen sink or a washtub with water. Gently put the boat on the water. Use a drinking straw to blow your boat across the water. The first boat to reach the other side wins.

Tin-Can Toss

Glue six tin cans together to form a triangle. Paint a number, from one to six, inside each can. If you use tempera paint, mix in some laundry detergent. Stand back and try to toss six buttons or pebbles into the cans. The player with the highest score wins.

Rabbit Race

Use a piece of stiff cardboard about 12 inches (30 cm) long. Draw a rabbit on the cardboard, as shown. Cut out the rabbit and color it on both sides. Punch a hole just below the head. Thread about 10 feet (3 m) of string through the hole. Tie one end of the string to a chair leg, just high enough for the rabbit's back legs to rest on the floor. Jerk the string to make the rabbit walk. When it reaches the chair, tilt it toward yourself and make it walk back to you. The first rabbit back wins.

Fun with Paper

Paper! It's easy to find and fun to work with. There are many different kinds of paper, but you will need only a few kinds to make the projects in this section.

Become a paper collector. Save old newspapers, magazines, paper plates, paper bags, and cardboard from cereal boxes and other cardboard containers. You will find many kinds of paper around the house. However, you may have to buy some special kinds, such as cellophane, construction, and tissue paper at a variety or art supply store.

Gather your supplies, learn a few simple skills, and you're ready to create with paper. If you've never worked with paper before, try the easy projects at the beginning of the section first. At the end of the section, you will find more ideas for paper projects.

Helpful hints

The following information will help you make the projects in this section. If a special skill is needed, the directions will tell you the page on which that skill is explained. For example: "Cut slits up to this line (see **slit,** page 37)." If you do not know how to slit paper, you will find directions on page 37.

Scissors, a **pencil,** and a **ruler** are the only tools you will need to do these paper projects. If you are left-handed, you can get left-handed scissors at an art supply store. **Transparent tape** and **white glue** are best for fastening paper together.

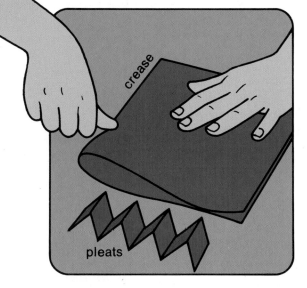

Fold paper by bending one edge over toward another edge. Then rub your thumb along the folded edge to make a sharp crease.

Pleat paper by folding it forward and backward in narrow strips.

Scoring helps you to fold stiff paper or to make a curved fold. Put a magazine or newspaper under the paper you are going to score. Draw a line to follow. Then go over the line with an old ball-point pen or the tip of your scissors. Press hard enough to make a mark in the paper.

Roll paper by wrapping it around itself or around a pencil.

Curl paper by pulling it across the edge of a ruler or the edge of a table.

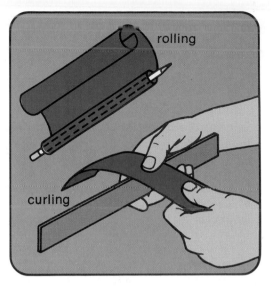
rolling

curling

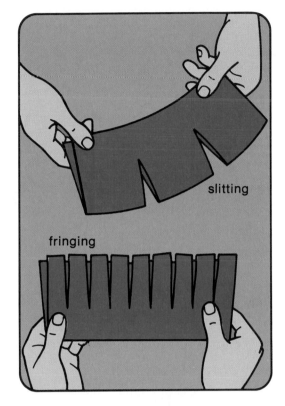
slitting

fringing

Slit paper by cutting into a folded edge. Do not cut all the way to the unfolded edge. The deeper you want the slit, the closer you must cut to the folded edge.

Fringe paper by cutting into an unfolded edge.

Inside cuts let you cut out an inner part of the paper. Bend the paper and make a little cut along the fold. Carefully poke one blade of your scissors through the cut. Hold the scissors still and move the paper as you cut.

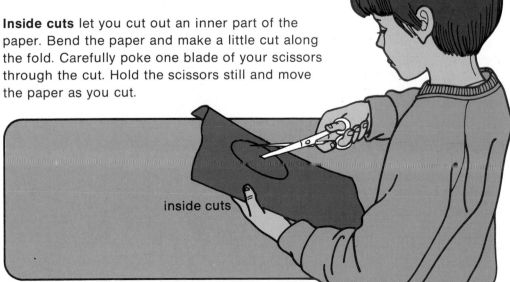
inside cuts

(continued on page 38)

Helpful hints

(continued from page 37)

To **square** a piece of paper, fold one corner to the opposite edge. The two edges of the paper should meet evenly. Cut off the leftover part.

The folded section is a **triangle.** Open the triangle up and you have a **square.** The piece you cut off is a **rectangle.**

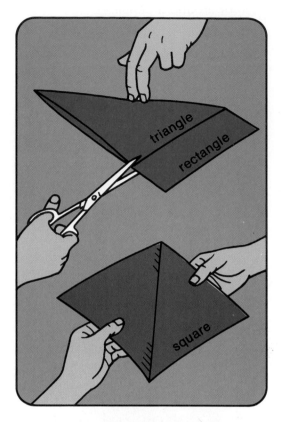

Circles can be made by drawing around any round object, such as a coin, a saucer, or the rim of a cup.

A **cone** is made from a circle. First, cut out a circle. Then cut from the edge to the center of the circle. Overlap the cut edges. Fasten them together and you have a shape called a cone. You can change the shape of the cone by cutting out triangular sections from the circle. The larger the section you cut out, the taller the cone will be.

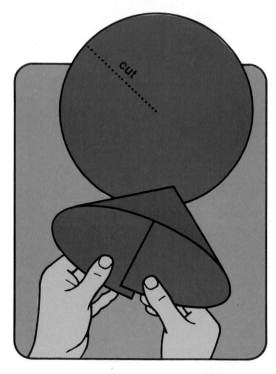

Paper collage

Materials

- **cardboard**
- **glue (white)**
- **paper**
- **scissors**

A collage is a picture made by gluing objects onto a flat surface. A collage can be as much fun to touch as it is to look at. For your collage, collect as many kinds and colors of paper as you can find. Try to get paper that is shiny, paper that is dull, paper that is rough, and paper that is smooth.

1 Cut or tear the paper so that you have pieces of different sizes and shapes.

2 Arrange the pieces of paper on a sheet of cardboard. Move the pieces of paper around until you have a design or a picture that you like.

3 When you like the way the design or picture looks, glue the pieces of paper in place.

Bug bookmark

Materials

- cardboard (thin)
- crayon (dark) or felt-tip pen
- glue (white)
- paper (two colors)
- ruler
- scissors

1 On the thin cardboard, draw a rectangle about as wide as your ruler and half as long.

Draw around the rim of a glass to make a circle at the top of the rectangle. This circle will be the bug.

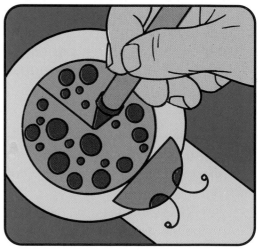

2 Now draw a smaller circle on colored paper. Cut out this circle. Glue it on top of the large circle.

Cut out a half-circle for the bug's head. Glue it to the large circle.

Now decorate the bug, as shown. Cut out the bookmark and it's ready to keep your place in a favorite book.

Fun fans

Materials

- **cardboard**
- **crayons or magic markers**
- **scissors**
- **transparent tape**
- **typing or notebook paper**

1 Place your bare foot (or your hand) on a piece of cardboard and draw around it. Cut out the shape and color both sides.

2 Roll a sheet of paper into a tight tube to make a handle (see **roll,** page 37). Tape the tube closed.

3 Tape one end of the tube to the fan and you are ready to keep cool on a hot day.

Now try making a great big hand or foot fan. You may have to roll two or three sheets of paper together to make a handle strong enough for the big fan.

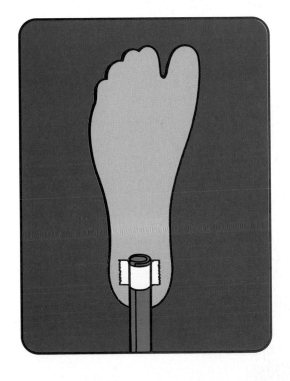

Japanese lantern

Materials

- **construction paper (two colors)**
- **ruler**
- **scissors**
- **transparent tape**

1 Cut a sheet of construction paper in half, the short way. Overlap the short ends of one half-sheet and tape them together to make a tube.

2 Fold a sheet of construction paper in half, the long way. Draw a straight line along the length of the paper, near the unfolded edges. Cut slits up to this line (see **slit,** page 37). Make the slits close together.

3 Unfold the slitted paper. Tape the end of one long edge to the top of the tube. Wrap the slit paper tightly around the tube. Let the ends overlap. Tape the top edge to the tube. Now tape the bottom edge of the slitted paper to the bottom edge of the tube.

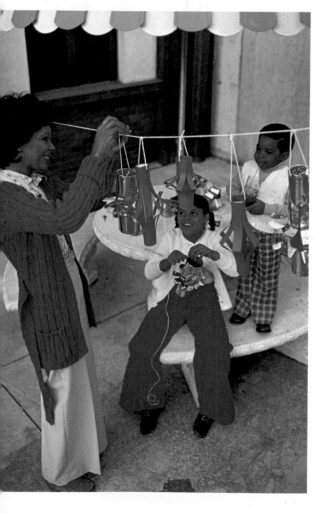

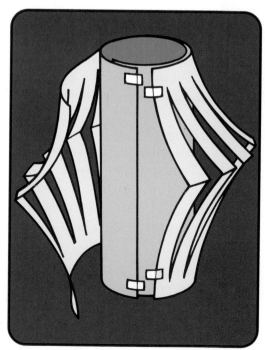

Magazine tower

Materials

- **glue (white)**
- **magazine**
- **scissors**
- **transparent tape**

1 Carefully tear out eight pages from a magazine. Roll each page into a tight tube, the long way (see **roll,** page 37). Tape the ends closed.

2 Place the eight tubes side by side so that the ends meet evenly. Tape the tubes together. Form the tubes into a circle and tape it closed.

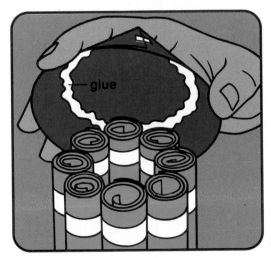

glue

3 Make a large cone from a magazine cover (see **cone,** page 38). To make a roof for the tower, glue the cone over the top of the tubes.

Woven mat

Materials

- newspaper (twelve sheets)
- scissors
- transparent tape

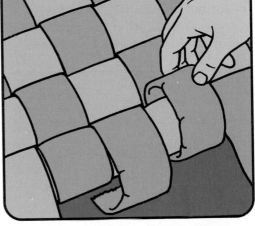

1 Fold twelve double-page sheets of newspaper into strips. Open each sheet and fold it in half the long way. Then fold it in half two more times. Press each strip with your hand to flatten it.

2 Place six of the strips side by side so that the ends meet evenly. Tape the strips down at one end to hold them in place.

3 Weave the other six strips over and under the strips you taped down, as shown. The first, third, and fifth strips should go *over* and under. The second, fourth, and sixth strips should go *under* and over.

4 When you finish weaving, untape the strips and push the rows together. Move the strips back and forth until the ends are even all around the mat.

5 Fold the loose ends of the strips over the edges of the mat and tuck them in. Turn the mat over and tuck in the loose ends on the other side.

Hanging shapes

Materials

- paper
- scissors
- thread
- transparent tape

1 Cut out a circle, a square, and a triangle. Draw lines on the shapes, as shown. Cut along these lines. Move the paper toward the scissors as you cut. Tape thread to each shape. Hang the shapes up and watch them twirl!

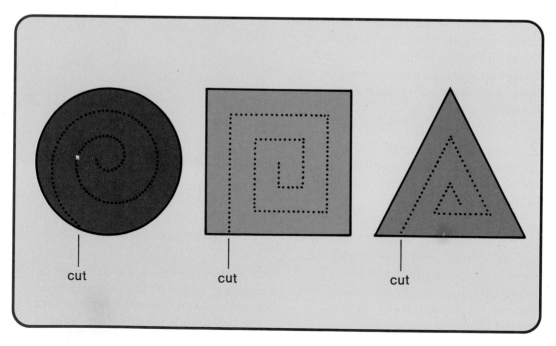

cut   cut   cut

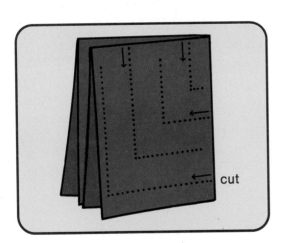

2 To make a fancier shape, fold a rectangle in half the long way. Now fold it in half again, the short way. Draw lines on the rectangle, as shown. Each line should start at a folded edge. Start two of the lines at the top and two at the side. End each line just before it reaches the other folded edge.

Now cut along these lines, as shown by the arrows. It's easier if you turn the paper as you cut.

3 Carefully unfold the rectangle. Hold it in the middle and shake it so that the strips fall below.

Tape a piece of thread to the shape. Hang the shape up and watch it twirl!

Stars and snowflakes

Materials

- **paper (large sheets)**
- **scissors**

1 Square your paper (see **square, page 38**). Cut off the rectangle, but leave the paper folded so that it is a triangle.

Fold the triangle in half, as shown by the dotted line in A.

2 Fold the triangle in half again, as shown in B.

3 Cut along a very slanted line, as shown in C. Open the paper and you have a four-pointed star.

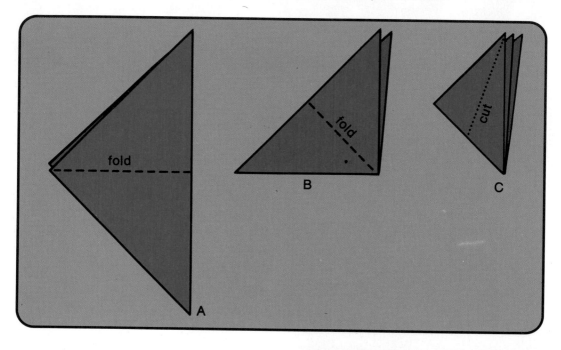

4 To make an eight-pointed star, repeat steps 1 and 2. Now fold the triangle once again, as shown. Then cut along the slanted line. Be sure to cut through all the folds. Open the paper and you have an eight-pointed star.

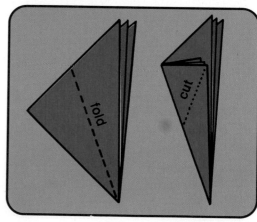

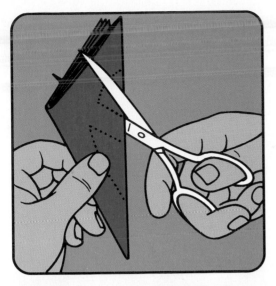

5 To make a snowflake, first make a four-pointed or an eight-pointed star. Keep the paper folded. Cut designs along each edge. Then unfold the paper.

Stars and snowflakes make nice holiday decorations. You can tape or glue them to other paper projects. Or, you can make a small hole in them and hang them up with a piece of thread.

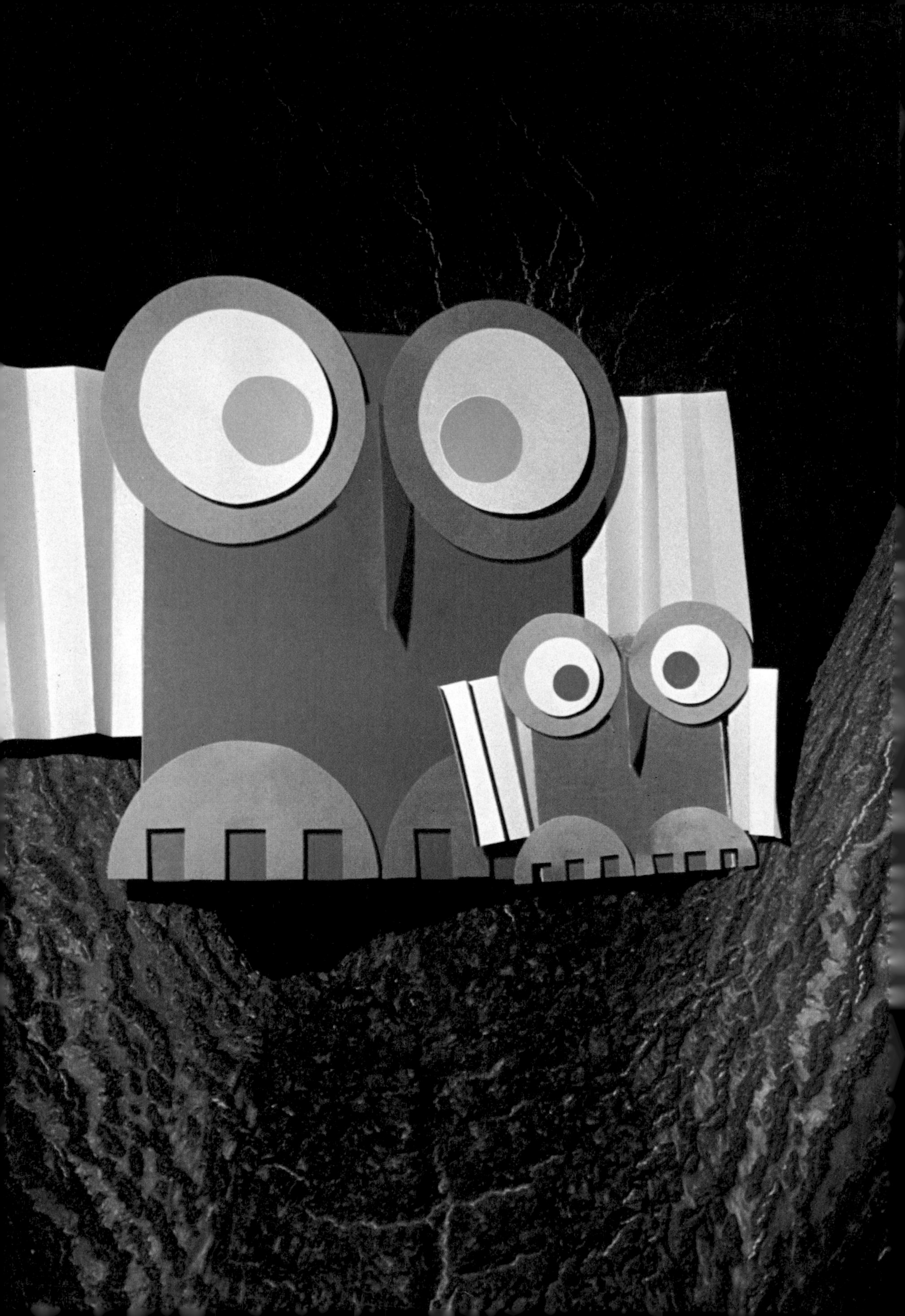

Ollie the owl

Materials

- **cardboard box (large)**
- **construction paper (three colors)**
- **glue (white)**
- **scissors**
- **transparent tape**

1 Find a large cardboard box (grocery stores usually have plenty). From the box, cut off a piece of cardboard about as long as your arm and as wide as this page.

2 Divide the piece of cardboard into three equal parts by drawing two straight lines on it, as shown. Score the cardboard along these lines (see **scoring,** page 36).

Now fold the cardboard along the scored lines until the two ends meet. Tape the ends together. This will be Ollie's body.

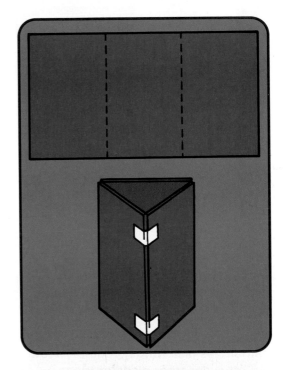

3 From the cardboard box, cut a long strip about as wide as your thumb. Cut this strip into eighteen small pieces. Glue three of the pieces together to make a thick stack. Make six of these stacks.

(continued on page 52)

Ollie the owl

(continued from page 51)

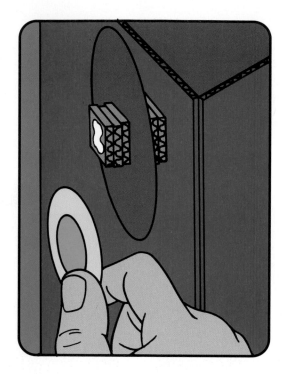

4 Cut out six circles (two large, two medium, and two small) from construction paper. Use a different color for each size. These circles will be Ollie's eyes.

To make the first part of the eyes, glue a cardboard stack on both sides of each large circle. Then put glue on one of the stacks on each of the circles. Glue these stacks near the top of Ollie's body.

To make the rest of the eyes, glue the medium-sized circles to the stacks on the large circles. Now glue the small circles on top of the medium-sized circles.

5 To make Ollie's claws, cut out a large circle from construction paper. Cut the circle in half.

Fringe the straight edges of the half-circles (see **fringe,** page 37). Now cut off every other piece of fringe.

Glue a cardboard stack to one side of each half-circle. Now glue the stacks near the bottom of Ollie's body.

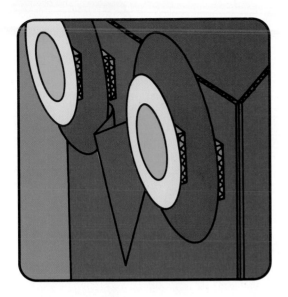

6 To make Ollie's nose, cut out a triangle from construction paper (see **triangle,** page 38). Fold the triangle in half. Open it up a little. Then glue the edges of the triangle between Ollie's eyes.

7 To make the wings, cut a sheet of construction paper in half. Pleat each half, the short way (see **pleat,** page 36). Then glue a pleated half-sheet to each side of Ollie's body.

Stained-glass fish

Materials

- construction paper (black)
- cellophane or tissue paper (different colors)
- pencil or crayon (light color)
- scissors
- transparent tape or white glue

1 Draw a fish on a piece of black construction paper. (Or, if you want, you can make up your own design.) Now draw several designs inside the fish. Be sure to draw the inside designs big enough so that you can cut them out easily.

2 Cut out the fish. Now cut out the inside designs (see **inside cuts,** page 37).

3 Arrange small pieces of colored cellophane or tissue paper over the cut-out spaces until you like what you see.

4 Tape or glue the pieces of cellophane or tissue paper over the cut-out spaces.

Hold the fish up to a window or a lamp and watch the colors light up!

Paper-plate mask

Materials

- crayons, felt-tip pens, or magic markers
- glue (white)
- paper plate (large)
- scissors
- string

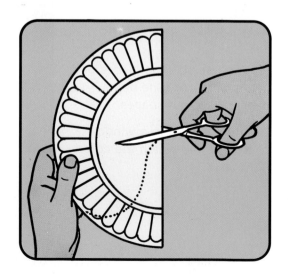

1 Fold a paper plate in half. Draw a line on the plate, as shown. Cut along this line. Save both parts of the plate.

2 Unfold the large part of the plate. Hold it against your face, with the bottom of the plate away from you. Use a crayon to make a light mark where the eye holes should go. Take the plate away from your face and cut out the eye holes (see **inside cuts**, page 37).

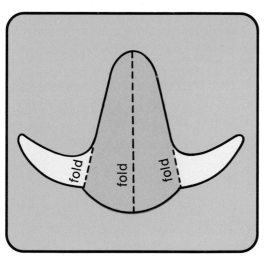

3 Use the small part of the plate for the nosepiece. Fold the nosepiece in half. Then fold the ends forward.

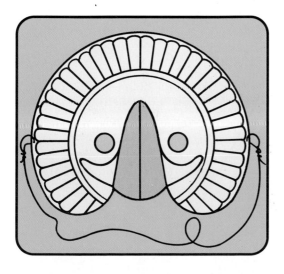

4 Open the nosepiece a little. Glue the folded ends on each side of the nose opening.

5 Attach string to hold the mask on. Punch a hole on each side edge of the mask. Cut a piece of string long enough to go around your head. Tie the ends of the string to the holes.

Use crayons, felt-tip pens, or magic markers to decorate your mask.

Color fortuneteller

Materials

- crayons, felt-tip pens, or magic markers
- paper (plain)
- scissors

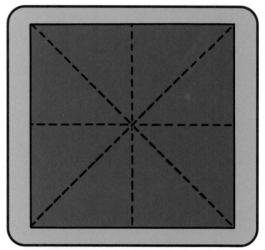

1 Square a sheet of paper (see **square,** page 38). Fold the square, as shown by the dashed lines. Be sure to make sharp creases on all the folds for this project.

2 Open the paper and fold each corner into the center. Keep the paper folded. Turn it over and fold each corner into the center again.

3 Each of the four corner flaps has two sections. Color each of these eight sections a different color.

Print the name of a career, such as artist, writer, nurse, doctor, singer, and so on, in each section.
Pick any eight careers you like.

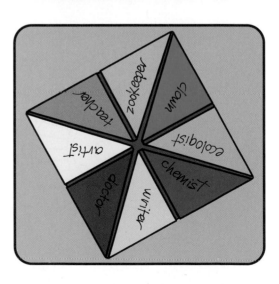

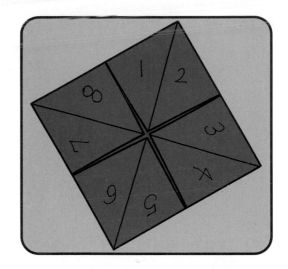

4 Turn the paper over. In each of the eight sections on this side, write a number from 1 to 8.

5 Fold the paper in half, with the colored career flaps on the inside. Hold the paper in both hands and push your hands together. Open the numbered flaps so they form cones.

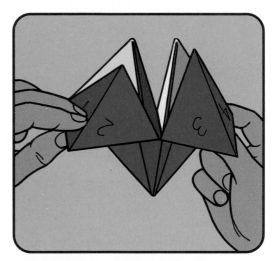

6 Hold the fortuneteller between the thumb and first finger of each hand. To see one group of careers, press the cones together and move your hands back and forth. To see the other group of careers, keep your hands together and open and close your fingers.

7 To tell a fortune, ask a friend to pick a number from 1 to 8. Open and close the fortuneteller this number of times. Then show your friend the career behind the number. This is what he or she will grow up to be.

On your own

Here are more things you can make with paper.

crumpled paper-sculpture picture

corrugated-paper popcorn holder

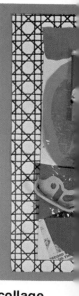

collage

paper-plate totem pole

game cube

vase and flowers

Paint and Print

How can you tell a story without using words? If you guessed "I can paint a picture," you're right! Paint talks. With paint you can tell about the places you've visited, the things you've seen, and the people you've met. Or, you can tell about what goes on in your imagination.

When you paint a story, there are lots of ways to use the paint. The projects in this section will show you some of them. You'll learn how to mix colors and how to paint with brushes, strings, your fingers, and other things. You'll find out how you can use potatoes and other objects to print pictures. And you'll discover the fun of making rubbings. Along the way, you might even invent your own way to use paint.

Paint and print time is a little like show and tell time, only different. With paintings and prints, you can "tell" stories you make up as well as show things that are real. So look around you. Or have a dream. Find a story to tell. Then paint or print or rub a picture.

Helpful hints

The following information will help you make some of the projects in this section. If a special skill is needed, the directions will tell you the page on which that skill is explained. For example: "Make a stamp pad (see **stamp pad**, page 66)." If you do not know how to make a stamp pad, you will find directions on page 66.

Before you start to paint or print, cover your work area with several layers of newspaper. Cover yourself with an apron, or an old shirt put on backwards. Keep a sponge or an old rag handy to wipe up any spills or spatters.

A **brush** is a basic tool used in painting. Paintbrushes come in different sizes. Some are soft and some are stiff. It's a good idea to have a large brush and a small brush. You can buy a package of assorted brushes at a variety store.

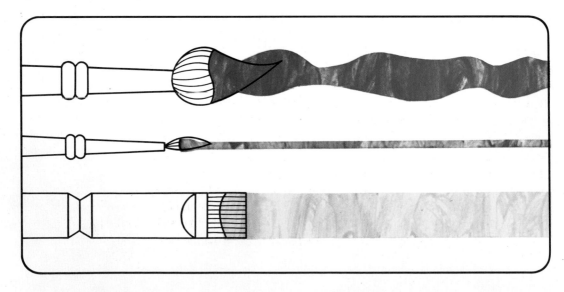

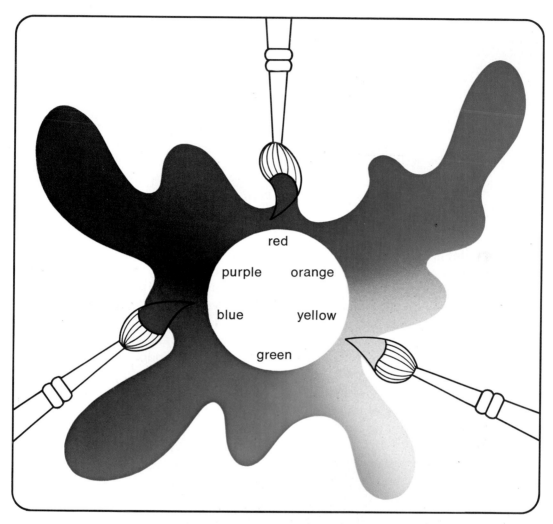

red

purple   orange

blue   yellow

green

Paint is the basic substance used in painting and printing. You can buy paint in many colors, but it's more fun to mix your own colors. Red, yellow, and blue are called **primary colors.** You can mix them together to make the **secondary colors,** green, purple, and orange.

Mix **yellow** and **blue** to make **green.**
Mix **red** and **blue** to make **purple.**
Mix **yellow** and **red** to make **orange.**

Mix your paints in small milk cartons, deep jar lids, empty juice cans, or other containers. Be sure to have a container of water handy to clean brushes and other painting tools.

When mixing colors, always add the darker color to the lighter color. Add a little at a time, until you have the color you want. To darken a color, add black. To lighten a color, add white.

(continued on page 66)

Helpful hints

(continued from page 65)

Tempera paint is the easiest paint to use for painting and printing. Tempera paint comes in liquid and powder form. You can buy small bottles of liquid tempera paint at a variety store. You may have to thin the paint with a little water. Powdered tempera paint can be bought at an art supply store. Mix powdered paint with water until it is creamy. Add a few drops of liquid starch to make the paint last longer.

Finger paint is thicker than tempera paint. You can buy finger paint at an art supply store, or you can make your own. To make finger paint, mix one cup of powdered tempera paint with one cup of liquid laundry starch. If you do not have tempera paint, you can mix two tablespoons of food coloring with the starch.

A **stamp pad** is a basic tool used in printing. To make a stamp pad, place a flat sponge or several layers of paper toweling on a shallow dish or a thick layer of newspaper. The pad can be any shape, but it should be larger than the object with which you are going to print. Pour a little paint in the center of the pad. Spread the paint until it seeps into the pad. Your stamp pad is ready to use.

Brush painting

Materials

- containers (four)
- newspaper (want-ad section)
- paintbrushes (large)
- tempera paint
  (blue, red, yellow)
- water

Before you begin this project, cover your work area with layers of newspaper. Cover yourself with an old shirt.

1 Pour each paint color into a separate container. Mix a little water with each color. The paint should be thin enough to flow easily from the brush, but thick enough to cover the print on the paper.

Fill another container with water. Place the paints and water where you can reach them easily.

2 Spread out a large sheet of newspaper from the want-ad section. The close print in this section of the paper will give you an even background for your painting.

3 Dip a paintbrush into the blue paint. Spread the paint in wide strokes on the newspaper. Now try making narrow lines of color with the tip of the brush. Dab the brush on the paper. Swish it around. See how many different ways you can use the brush.

4 Clean your brush in water, or get a clean one. This time, dip the brush into the yellow paint. Brush the paint over the paper. Spread some of the yellow paint on top of the blue paint and watch what happens.

5 Now place a clean sheet of newspaper on your work area. Try mixing other colors together. Remember the colors you like and how you made them. Be sure to clean your brush in water each time you use a new color.

Finger painting

Materials

- **containers (plastic)**
- **food coloring or powdered tempera paint**
- **laundry starch (liquid)**
- **newspaper**
- **shelf paper (shiny)**
- **sponge**
- **water**

Before you start this project, cover your work area with layers of newspaper. Cover yourself with an old shirt.

1 Fill three or four plastic containers half full with liquid starch. Stir a little food coloring or powdered tempera paint into the starch.

2 Cut off a large piece of shelf paper. Place it shiny side up on a layer of newspaper. Wet the shelf paper all over with a sponge.

3 Place a spoonful of paint on the wet shelf paper. Spread the paint all over the paper with your hands. Now use your fingers, your wrists, the sides of your hands, your closed fists, or even your fingernails to make designs on the paper.

4 Sprinkle a few drops of water on the paper when the paint gets too sticky. You can erase a design anytime you like. Simply add a little water and spread the paint over the paper again.

5 When you have finished painting, lift the picture by two corners. Put it on a layer of newspaper to dry.

Straw painting

Before you start this project, cover your work area with layers of newspaper. Cover yourself with an old shirt.

1 Use a spoon to place a drop of paint on a piece of shiny shelf paper.

2 Place one end of a drinking straw near the drop of paint. Blow gently through the other end of the straw to spread out the paint. Move the paper around as you blow. The paint will spread out in different directions. Now place a few drops of the other colors on the paper and blow them around.

3 When you finish your picture, let it dry on a layer of newspaper. Some of the blown designs may look like trees or animals. Draw around these shapes with a felt-tip pen so they stand out.

String painting

Materials

- containers (three)
- paper
- spoons (three)
- string
- tempera paint (three colors)

Before you start this project, cover your work area with layers of newspaper. Cover yourself with an old shirt.

1 Use a spoon to scoop some paint into a container. Use a different spoon and a different container for each color.

2 Cut three pieces of string, each about half as long as your arm. Hold a piece of string by one end and dip the other end into one of the colors. Be sure the paint covers the string. Hang the clean end of the string over the edge of the container. Dip the other pieces of string into the other containers the same way.

3 Pull one of the strings out of the paint. Hold the string by the clean end and drop the rest of it on a sheet of paper. Lift the string up again and drop it on another part of the paper. The paint-covered string will make wiggly designs on the paper. When the string gets too dry, dip it into the paint again. Do the same thing with the strings in the other colors.

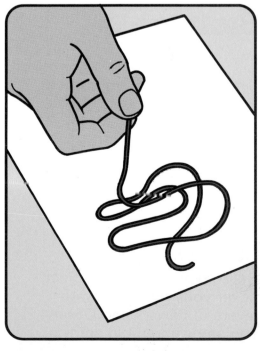

4 Now try folding a piece of paper in half, with the string inside. Press the folded paper gently with your hand and pull the string out of the paper. Open the paper up and see what kind of design you have made. Hang your string paintings on the wall, or use them to make greeting cards.

Blottos

Materials

- **construction paper**
- **spoons (three)**
- **tempera paint
  (liquid, three colors)**

Before you start this project, cover your work area with layers of newspaper. Cover yourself with an old shirt.

1 Fold a sheet of construction paper in half. Make a sharp crease along the fold. Then open up the paper and lay it flat.

2 Use the spoons to sprinkle a little of each color paint on one-half of the construction paper. Now fold the paper in half along the fold line, with the paint inside. Press the paper down smoothly with your hand.

3 Open up the paper and see what kind of design you have made. Leave the design as it is, or add more paint and fold the paper again.

For your next picture, try sprinkling the paint in different places.

Rubbings

Materials

- coins
- crayons
- paper (thin)
- scissors

1 Place a coin on a flat surface. Place a piece of thin paper on top of the coin. Hold the paper in place with one hand and rub the side of a crayon over the paper. As you rub, the design on the coin will appear on the paper.

Move the paper and make another rubbing of the coin. Place other coins next to the one under the paper and continue rubbing.

2 Look around the house and outdoors for other patterns to rub. Window screens and pieces of wood have interesting patterns. Make a collection of rubbings, cut them out, and mount them in a scrapbook.

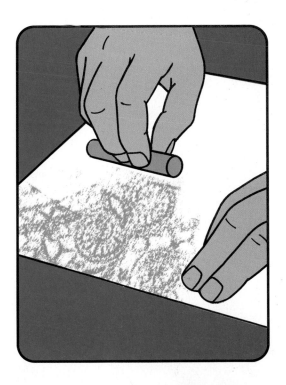

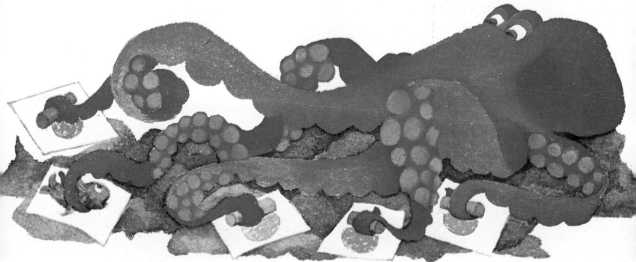

Pleat and dye prints

Materials

- containers (three)
- food coloring (blue, red, yellow)
- newspaper
- paper towels (white)
- water

Before you start this project, cover your work area with layers of newspaper. Cover yourself with an old shirt.

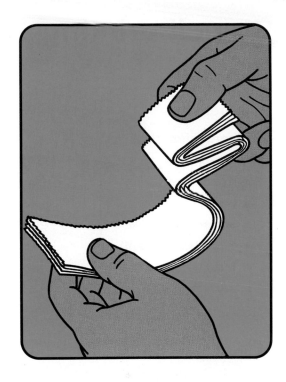

1 Pour a little of each food color into different containers. Add a little water to each color.

2 Tear off a paper towel. Pleat the paper towel (see **pleat,** page 36) in large, even strips, the long way. Keeping the towel folded, pleat it again, the short way.

3 Hold the pleated towel in the middle to keep the pleats together. Dip a corner into one of the food colors. The color will spread quickly, so take the towel out as soon as the color starts to spread.

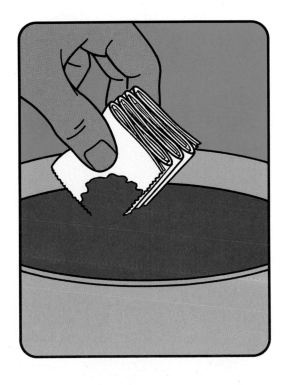

Now dip a second corner into another color. Then dip a third corner into the last color.

4 Unfold the towel very carefully and lay it on a layer of newspaper to dry. When it is dry, you can use it as gift-wrapping paper. Or, glue it to a piece of construction paper to make a greeting card.

Stencil printing

Materials

- **cardboard (thin)**
- **felt-tip pen**
- **newspaper**
- **paper**
- **scissors**
- **tape (transparent)**
- **tempera paint**
- **toothbrush (old)**

Before you start this project, cover your work area with layers of newspaper. Cover yourself with an old shirt.

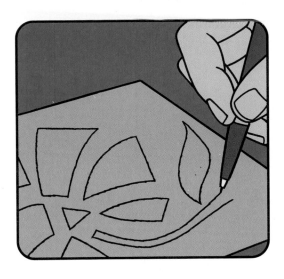

1 Use a felt-tip pen to draw a simple design on a piece of cardboard. If your design has more than one part, draw each part separately, as shown. Be sure to leave space between all the parts of the design.

2 Cut out each part of the design (see **inside cuts,** page 37). You now have a piece of cardboard with holes in it. This is your stencil. You will paint through the holes in the stencil.

3 Take a piece of blank paper and put it on a layer of newspaper. Place the stencil on top of the paper and tape it down on all four sides. The paper will show through the holes.

4 Hold a toothbrush in one hand. Use a finger of the other hand to dab a little paint on the bristles of the toothbrush.

Hold the toothbrush over one of the holes in the stencil. Now run your finger over the paint-covered bristles. Be sure to move your finger toward you, so that the paint will spatter away from you. The paint will spatter onto the paper through the holes in the stencil. Do the same thing over each of the holes.

5 When you finish spattering paint, carefully untape the stencil and lift it off the paper. Your design is now on the paper, and you have a stencil print to hang in your room.

Gadget printing

Materials

- jar lid
- paper clips
- pencil
- printing pad
- shelf paper

Before you start this project, cover your work area with layers of newspaper. Cover yourself with an old shirt.

1 Make a stamp pad (see **stamp pad**, page 66).

2 Cut off a large piece of shelf paper. Place it shiny side up on a layer of newspaper. You will print on the shiny side of the shelf paper.

3 A jar lid is a good object to start printing with. Press the rim of the lid on the stamp pad. Make sure the rim is covered with paint.

4 Press the paint-covered rim on the shelf paper. Press down firmly. Do not let the lid move around on the paper. Carefully lift up the lid. You now have a print of the rim on the paper. Make two or three more prints before you press the lid on the stamp pad again.

5 Print with the eraser end of a pencil, the same way you printed with the jar lid.

6 Now try printing with a paper clip. Bend up the small, inside part of the paper clip. Hold the small part of the clip and press the large part on the stamp pad. Now press the large part of the clip on the shelf paper.

7 Try printing with other objects you find around the house, such as bottle caps, cookie cutters, forks, and empty spools. Look around outdoors for rocks, sticks, and leaves to print with.

Potato prints

Before you start this project, cover your work area with layers of newspaper. Cover yourself with an old shirt.

1 Ask a grown-up to help you cut a potato in half.

2 Pour some thick tempera paint onto several layers of paper toweling. Use just enough paint to cover the toweling.

3 Cut off a large piece of shelf paper. Place it shiny side down on a layer of newspaper. You will print on the dull side of the paper.

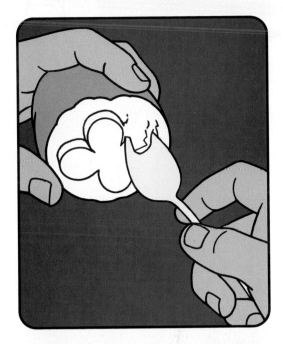

4 Take one of the potato halves. Use a pencil to scratch a simple design in the center of the cut side of the potato.

Use the tip of a spoon to scoop out the parts around your design. Only the raised parts of the potato will print.

5 Dip the raised design on the potato into the paint. Now press the design onto the shelf paper. You can press the design onto the paper two or three times before you have to dip it in the paint again. Use the other half of the potato to make a different design.

6 You can also print with half of a grapefruit, a lemon, or an orange. Ask a grown-up to help you scoop out each section of the fruit. Try to leave the thin skin, or membrane, between each section. Squeeze out as much of the juice as you can. Then wipe out each section of the fruit with a paper towel. Dip the cut part of the fruit into the paint. Then print the same way you printed with the potato.

Raised
cardboard prints

Before you start this project, cover your
work area with layers of newspaper.
Cover yourself with an old shirt.

Materials

- cardboard (thick)
- containers
- glue (white)
- paintbrush
- scissors
- starch (liquid)
- tempera paint
- typing or
  shelf paper

1 Draw a few simple shapes on a piece of thick cardboard. Cut out these shapes.

2 Cut a piece of cardboard about the size of this page. Arrange the cut-out shapes on this piece of cardboard. When you like the way you have arranged the shapes, glue them in place.

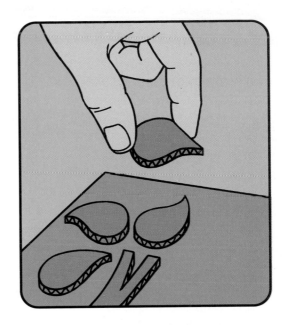

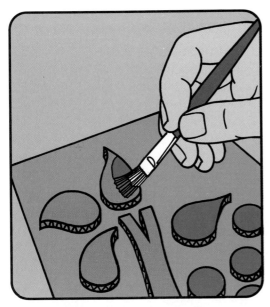

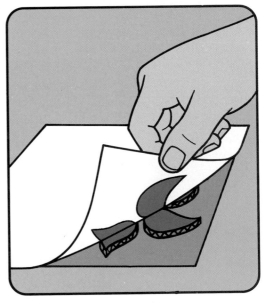

3 Mix some tempera paint and liquid starch in a plastic container. Use a paintbrush to cover each cardboard shape with a thick layer of paint. Use one color for all the shapes, or paint some of them different colors. If you want to print with more than one color, use a different container for each color.

4 Place a piece of typing or shelf paper on top of the paint-covered shapes. Rub your hand over the paper, pressing down hard. Hold the paper by one corner and peel it off. You now have a print of the cardboard shapes.

On your own

Here are more things you can do with paint.

painted cardboard screen

building cards

playing cards

clay-pot figure

painted-carton mask

Styrofoam block prints

Papier-Mâché

Here's a riddle! What's hard as a rock, light as a feather, is made from something you throw away every day, and will last for many years?

It's a hard riddle, but the answer will lead you into a whole new world of make and do. The answer is papier-mâché.

Papier-mâché has a fancy French name, but it is really ordinary newspaper mixed with a special paste. It's easy to make, easy to mold, and easy to turn into all kinds of interesting and beautiful objects.

What can you make with papier-mâché? Just about anything! You can make necklaces and trays, a happy horse and a funny puppet, and a special Mexican surprise to play with at a party. So turn the page and see how easy it is to make and do with papier-mâché.

Helpful hints

The following information will help you make some of the projects in this section. If a special skill is needed, the directions will tell you the page on which that skill is explained. For example: "Make some papier-mâché pulp (see **papier-mâché pulp, page 89**)." If you do not know how to make papier-mâché pulp, you will find directions on page 89.

Papier-mâché is French for chewed paper, or paper pulp. When wet, papier-mâché is easily shaped. When dry, it is hard and strong and can be painted.

Strip papier-mâché is made by tearing sheets of newspaper into narrow strips about 1 inch (2.5 cm) wide. Tear the newspaper from the fold down. Cover the strips with papier-mâché paste by pulling each strip through the paste. Or, spread the paste on each strip with a paintbrush.

To cover an object with papier-mâché strips, paste on a layer of strips in one direction. Then paste on another layer of strips in the other direction, so that they go across the first layer. Smooth down all of the strips. Continue this way until you have put on four or more layers.

Papier-mâché pulp can be shaped like clay or used to cover objects. You can buy papier-mâché mix in variety stores or craft shops. This mix works best for pulp projects. Or, you can make pulp from old newspapers.

To make papier-mâché pulp, tear newspaper into pieces about 1 inch (2.5 cm) square. Fill a pail or large pan with the pieces of paper. Squeeze papier-mâché paste into the paper until the mixture feels like clay.

Or, ask a grown-up to help you make pulp with an electric beater or in a blender. Fill a pail half full with 1-inch (2.5-cm) square pieces of newspaper. Fill the pail with warm water and let the paper soak overnight. Then mix the paper and water with the beater. Squeeze out the water and place the pulp in a large container. Finally, squeeze papier-mâché paste into the pulp until the mixture feels like clay.

Papier-mâché paste is mixed with strip and pulp papier-mâché to get a hard finish. Here are three recipes for making this paste.

(1) Stir three parts water into one part flour until the mixture is smooth and creamy. To make the paste last longer, add a few drops of oil of wintergreen. You can buy this oil at a drugstore.

(2) Buy some wallpaper paste at a hardware store. Mix one part wallpaper paste with three parts water. Stir well and the paste is ready to use.

(3) Mix two parts white glue with one part warm water. Stir well and the paste is ready to use.

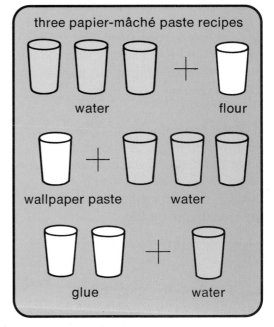

three papier-mâché paste recipes

water   flour

wallpaper paste   water

glue   water

To **dry** objects made of papier-mâché, leave them in an open place for two or more days. Or, ask a grown-up to dry the objects in an oven set to a temperature of about 150°F. (65°C). **Warning:** Projects made with balloons should not be dried in an oven.

Neck ornament

Materials

- **newspaper**
- **paintbrush**
- **papier-mâché pulp**
- **tempera paint**
- **yarn or string**

1 Make some papier-mâché pulp (see **papier-mâché pulp,** page 89). Drop two large spoonfuls of pulp on a thick layer of newspaper. Press and squeeze the pulp until it is smooth. Now roll the pulp into a ball. Flatten out the ball on the newspaper.

2 Poke two holes through the pulp near the top edge, as shown. Now press designs into the pulp with your finger. Press firmly, but do not go through the other side. Let the pulp dry (see **dry,** page 89).

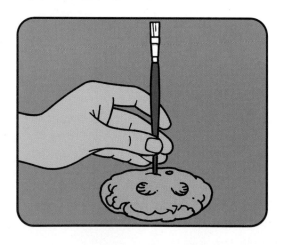

3 When the pulp is dry, paint designs on it with tempera paint. Paint one side at a time. When the one side is dry, paint the other side.

4 Cut a piece of yarn or string long enough to go around your neck. Place one end of the yarn through the holes you poked out in step 2. Pull the yarn through the holes and tie the ends around your neck. If you have enough pulp left over, try making earrings to match the neck ornament.

Small tray

Materials

- brick or heavy book
- meat or vegetable tray (plastic, cardboard, or styrofoam)
- paintbrushes
- paste
- strip papier-mâché
- tempera paint
- varnish

1 Find an empty meat or vegetable tray. Cover the tray with five or six layers of papier-mâché strips (see **strip papier-mâché**, page 88). Cover the front, back, and sides of the tray. Smooth the strips down around the corners of the tray.

Let the papier-mâché dry (see **dry,** page 89). To keep the tray from bending while it is drying, put a brick or heavy book in it. If you use a book, wrap it in plastic to keep it from getting wet.

2 When the papier-mâché is completely dry, paint the tray any color you like with tempera paint. You can also paint designs on the tray or paste colorful magazine cutouts on it.

3 When you finish decorating the tray, spread a thin coat of varnish on it with a paintbrush. The varnish will make the tray look shiny.

Horse

Materials

- glue (white)
- newspaper
- paintbrush
- papier-mâché pulp
- pipe cleaners or wire
- tempera paint
- yarn

1 Make a large supply of papier-mâché pulp (see **papier-mâché pulp,** page 89). You will use the pulp in step 3.

2 Twist three pipe cleaners together, as shown, to make the horse's body. Bend another pipe cleaner in half and shape it to make the horse's head and neck. Twist the end of the body pipe cleaner around the neck. Cover the pipe-cleaner horse with white glue to make it strong. Let it dry completely.

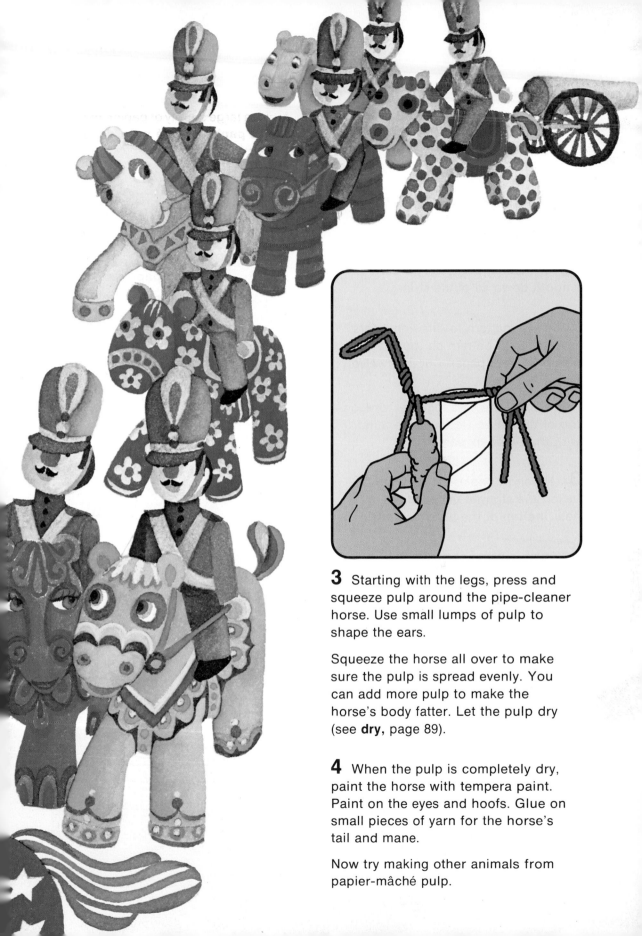

3 Starting with the legs, press and squeeze pulp around the pipe-cleaner horse. Use small lumps of pulp to shape the ears.

Squeeze the horse all over to make sure the pulp is spread evenly. You can add more pulp to make the horse's body fatter. Let the pulp dry (see **dry,** page 89).

4 When the pulp is completely dry, paint the horse with tempera paint. Paint on the eyes and hoofs. Glue on small pieces of yarn for the horse's tail and mane.

Now try making other animals from papier-mâché pulp.

Lion wall decoration

Materials

- **aluminum foil**
- **newspaper**
- **paintbrushes**
- **paper plate**
- **scissors**
- **strip papier-mâché**
- **tempera paint**
- **transparent tape**

1 Place a paper plate on a flat surface. Cover one side of the plate with two or three layers of papier-mâché strips (see **strip papier-mâché,** page 88). Be sure to smooth down all of the strips.

2 Draw a pattern for the lion's ears. Place the ear pattern on top of twelve pieces of newspaper. Cut out twelve ears.

Paste six of the ears together, one on top of the other. Do the same thing with the other six ears.

3 Use short papier-mâché strips to fasten the straight edges of the ears near the top of the plate, as shown.

4 Crush a piece of newspaper to make a shape for the lion's nose. Place the crushed paper in the center of the plate. To hold the nose in place, paste a layer of papier-mâché strips over the nose and part of the plate. Make sure that the strips cover the nose. Smooth down any bumpy parts with your fingers.

5 Cover the plate and the nose with three layers of papier-mâché strips. Follow the shape of the nose as you paste down the strips.

Let the papier-mâché dry (see **dry,** page 89). When it is completely dry, you can paint the mask with tempera paint. Be sure to paint on the lion's eyes and mouth.

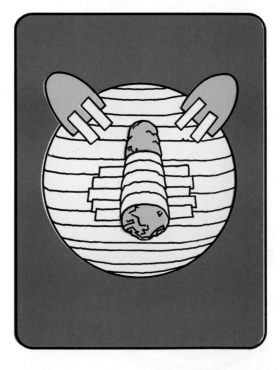

6 Cut off four narrow strips of aluminum foil for the lion's whiskers. Fold each strip the long way. Cut each strip in half. You now have eight strips.

Hold four of the strips together so that the ends overlap. Tape the ends together to make a set of whiskers. Do the same thing with the other four strips. Now tape a set of whiskers on each side of the nose.

7 Cut off two medium-sized strips of aluminum foil for the lion's mane. Carefully fringe, then roll each strip (see **fringe** and **roll,** page 37). Tape the fringed strips around the edge of the plate.

Tape a loop of string to the back of the plate and your mask is ready to hang on your wall or bulletin board.

Bottle figure

Materials

- bottle (plastic)
- newspaper
- paintbrushes
- sand or salt
- strip papier-mâché
- tempera paint
- yarn

1 Find an empty plastic bottle (a detergent bottle works well). Pour about two cupfuls of sand or salt into the bottle. This will keep the bottle from tipping over.

2 Tear a sheet of newspaper in half. Crush one piece of the newspaper into a small, tight ball. Place the ball in the center of the other piece of newspaper. Pick up the four corners and tightly twist them together to hold the ball in place. The ball will be the head for your bottle figure.

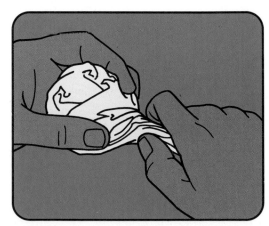

3 Push the twisted end of the newspaper into the opening at the top of the bottle. The ball should be the only part showing.

4 Paste four layers of papier-mâché strips over the ball and the top part of the bottle (see **strip papier-mâché,** page 88) to hold these parts together. Smooth the strips around the ball.

Cover the ball and the bottle with four more layers of strips. Let the strips dry (see **dry,** page 89).

5 When the figure is dry, you can paint the body, arms, face, and clothes with tempera paint. You can use small pieces of yarn for the hair.

When the paint dries, you can use your bottle figure as a paperweight or as a bookend.

Puppet head

Materials

- newspaper
- paintbrushes
- papier-mâché (pulp and strip)
- tempera paint
- toilet-paper tube
- transparent tape
- yarn

1 To form the puppet's head, crumple a sheet of newspaper into a ball. Put a piece of tape around the ball.

2 Cut an empty toilet-paper tube in half. Tape the tube to the ball.

3 Cover the ball and the tube with two layers of strip papier-mâché (see **strip papier-mâché,** page 88). Let the papier-mâché stiffen for about four hours.

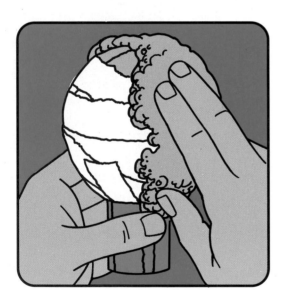

4 Cover the ball and the tube with a thin layer of papier-mâché pulp (see **papier-mâché pulp,** page 89). Press more pulp around the place where the ball and the tube meet. Smooth the pulp with your hands.

Use small pieces of pulp to shape the puppet's ears, nose, mouth, and eyes. Let the papier-mâché dry (see **dry,** page 89).

5 Now paint the puppet head with tempera paint. Glue pieces of yarn to the head to make hair. Add any other decorations you like.

Attach a piece of cloth to the tube with a rubber band. Place your hand under the cloth. Poke one or two fingers through the tube. You're ready to put on a puppet show.

Gooey bird

1 Make some papier-mâché pulp (see **papier-mâché pulp,** page 89). You will use the pulp in step 3.

2 To make the gooney bird's body, blow up a balloon and tie the neck tightly. Cover the balloon with seven or eight layers of papier-mâché strips (see **strip papier-mâché,** page 88). Let the papier-mâché dry (see **dry,** page 89).

3 Use two plastic drinking straws for the bird's legs. Cover each straw with two or three layers of papier-mâché strips. Wrap the strips around the straws and let dry.

Use a pencil to poke two small holes into one end of the bird's body. Push a straw into each hole. Now press some papier-mâché pulp around each hole to hold the straws in place. Dab a little white glue around the edges of the pulp to make sure the legs stay in place. Let the pulp dry completely.

4 For the bird's beak, make a cone from a sheet of newspaper (see **cone,** page 38). Cover the cone with two layers of papier-mâché strips. Paste short strips around the outside edge of the cone. Then paste the loose ends of the strips to the body, as shown. Paste on more papier-mâché strips to hold the beak in place.

Materials

- balloon (small)
- cardboard (heavy)
- drinking straws (two, plastic)
- glue (white)
- paintbrushes
- paper (gift-wrapping and construction)
- papier-mâché (pulp and strip)
- pebbles
- tempera paint
- transparent tape

5 Draw two large feet on a piece of heavy cardboard. Cut out the feet. Place a few pebbles on each foot. The added weight will help the bird stand up. Now cover each foot with a layer of papier-mâché pulp. Be sure that the pebbles are covered. Let the pulp dry for about three or four hours.

6 While the pulp is drying, you can make the bird's top feathers. Fringe and curl a strip of construction paper (see **fringe** and **curl,** page 37). Roll the curled strip into a tube and tape it closed.

Now paste short papier-mâché strips around the uncurled edge of the tube, as you did for the cone in step 4. Paste the loose ends of these strips to the top of the bird's body.

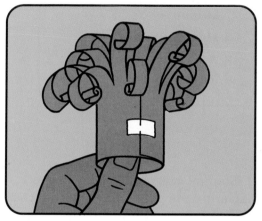

7 When the pulp is almost dry, push the straws into the center of each papier-mâché foot. Press a little pulp and dab some glue around the straws to hold them in place. Lean the bird against a wall, or prop his beak on a box. Let the pulp dry.

8 To make the bird's leg feathers, fringe and curl two long strips of gift-wrapping paper. Cover one leg with a thin layer of paste. Starting at the bottom with the fringed edge pointing down, wind and press the strip around the leg. Then paste and feather the other leg.

When the bird is dry, you can decorate it with tempera paint.

Turtle piñata

Materials

- **balloon (large)**
- **candy (wrapped)**
- **glue (white)**
- **paintbrushes**
- **papier-mâché (pulp and strip)**
- **string**
- **tempera paint**
- **toilet-paper tubes (three)**

A piñata is a papier-mâché or clay pot which is shaped like an animal or person and filled with candy. Children in Mexico and other Latin-American countries enjoy playing with piñatas around holiday time.

1 Start by making a large supply of papier-mâché pulp (see **papier-mâché pulp,** page 89). You will use the pulp in steps 5 and 6.

2 For the turtle's body, blow up a large balloon and tie the neck. Cover the balloon with two or three layers of papier-mâché strips (see **strip papier-mâché,** page 88).

3 To make the legs, cut two empty toilet-paper tubes on a slant, as shown. Cover each tube with a layer of papier-mâché strips.

Attach the legs to the body, one at a time. Place each leg so that the slanted edge rests flat against the body. Use short papier-mâché strips to fasten the legs to the body, as shown. Paste on more papier-mâché strips to hold all the pieces in place.

4 To make the turtle's neck, cut another toilet-paper tube on a slant as you did for the legs. Cover one of the tubes with a layer of papier-mâché strips. Fasten the neck to one end of the turtle's body the same way you attached the legs in step 3. Let the strips dry (see **dry,** page 89).

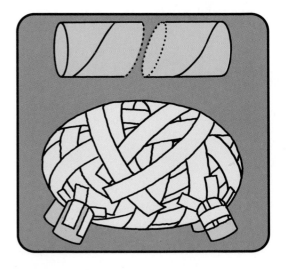

7 Ask a grown-up to cut an opening as big as your fist in the bottom of the turtle. Place handfuls of wrapped candy inside the turtle. Then paste a layer of papier-mâché strips over the opening. Let the strips dry.

5 Use the papier-mâché pulp you made in step 1 to make the turtle's head. Roll two large spoonfuls of pulp into a ball. Place the ball in the open end of the neck. Press pulp around the head and neck.

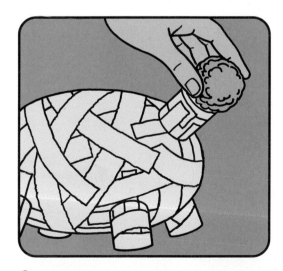

6 Cover the neck, legs, and the top and sides of the body with pulp. Do not cover the bottom of the turtle's body with pulp. Do not pick up the turtle as you work. Let the pulp dry for two or more days.

8 If you want to hang the piñata, you'll need to attach a string. To do this, poke a small hole in the top of the turtle's body. Push one end of a long piece of string into the hole. Press a little pulp around the hole. To make sure the string doesn't slip out, dab a little white glue around the hole. Let the pulp and the glue dry.

Decorate your piñata with tempera paint or colored paper. To find out how to use your piñata, turn to the section titled "Come to My Party."

On your own

Here are more things you
can make with papier-mâché.

monster mask

finger puppets

doll cradle

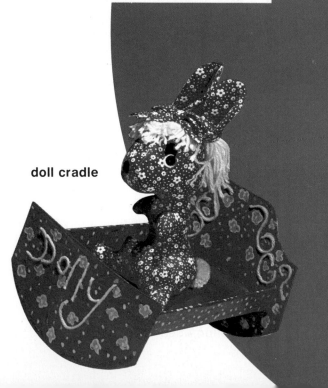

totem pole

piggy bank

bull mask

marionette

Let's Play with Clay

It's wonderful to play with clay! It feels good to touch, and it's fun to push and squeeze into different shapes.

You can make anything and everything out of clay. You can make pots and people and puppies and parades. Would you like to model a circus, a zoo, or a supermarket? How about modeling a funny bone, a Martian city, or a secret place? You can model shapes that look like something real, or you can model shapes that don't look like anything you ever saw.

You can model clay by yourself. Or you can ask your friends to help you work on a big project. There is no right or wrong way to play with clay. Whatever you do and whatever you make is right for you.

The projects in this section will show you just some of the things you can make from clay. You can make many more. Just take some clay, add a little bit of imagination, then roll, pat, pinch, and flatten as your fingers tell you to.

Helpful hints

The following information will help you to make the projects in this section. If a special skill is needed, the directions will tell you the page on which that skill is explained. For example: "Roll a lump of clay into a coil (see **coil**, page 110)." If you do not know how to make a coil, you will find directions on page 110.

You do not need any **special tools** to work with clay. Your hands and fingers are your best tools. To do things your fingers can't do, you can use objects found around the house. Toothpicks, orange sticks, combs, string, pencils, a fork, a spoon, a knife, hairpins, cookie cutters, and a rolling pin are all good tools to use.

When you play with clay, it's a good idea to use a **work base**. It lets you turn your model without picking it up. A wooden board, a piece of heavy cardboard, or a sheet of paper makes a good work base.

Clay is a soft material that is easy to shape. There are several different kinds of clay. Some you can buy in art stores, and others you can make in your kitchen.

Hardening clay is ordinary earth clay. You can buy this clay in art stores and hobby shops. It is the best clay for modeling.

If it begins to crack while modeling, hardening clay should be brushed or moistened with water. Pieces of this clay must be scored (see **score**, page

111) and moistened with water before they will stick together.

Hardening clay dries to a stiff, hard finish. Models made from this clay are very strong. If handled with care, they will not break easily. When dry, this clay can be painted with tempera paint (see **tempera paint**, page 66).

Modeling clay, or Plasticine, is an artificial clay often used in place of hardening clay. You can buy this clay in art stores, hobby shops, and variety stores.

You can stick and smooth pieces of modeling clay together with your fingers. No special treatment is needed.

Modeling clay does not dry or harden. It can be used many times. The objects you make from modeling clay will keep their shape until you reroll the clay to make something else. But, modeling clay cannot be painted.

Chemical clay is a clay substitute you can make in your kitchen. Pieces of this clay must be moistened with water before they will stick together.

Chemical clay dries to a stonelike finish. Models made from chemical clay are very strong. They will not break easily. When dry, this clay can be painted with tempera paints (see **tempera paint**, page 66).

Chemical clay
(makes a lump of clay about the size of a softball)

- $\frac{1}{2}$ cup cornstarch
- 1 cup salt
- $\frac{3}{4}$ cup water
- cooking pot
- old pie tin or aluminum foil
- mixing spoon

1 Mix 1 cup of salt and $\frac{1}{2}$ cup of cornstarch in the cooking pot.

2 Slowly stir in $\frac{3}{4}$ cup of water. Keep stirring until the mixture is smooth.

3 Ask a grown-up to cook and stir the mixture over low heat until it is stiff, like mashed potatoes. This will take about two or three minutes.

4 Spoon the mixture onto a pie tin or a piece of aluminum foil. Let cool for about ten minutes.

5 When the mixture is cool enough to handle, press and squeeze it until it feels like clay. This will take about three or four minutes.

6 To store unused chemical clay, wrap it in wax paper. It will keep for several days. If chemical clay becomes too sticky, squeeze a little water into the clay.

(continued on page 110)

Helpful hints

(continued from page 109)

Kitchen clay is a clay substitute you can make in your kitchen. Pieces of this clay must be moistened with water before they will stick together.

After several days, kitchen clay dries to a stiff, hard finish. Models made from kitchen clay are very strong. If handled with care, they will not break easily. When dry, kitchen clay can be painted with tempera paint (see **tempera paint**, page 66).

Kitchen clay

(makes a lump of clay about the size of a softball)

- $1\frac{1}{2}$ cups flour
- $\frac{1}{2}$ cup salt
- $\frac{1}{4}$ cup vegetable oil (or a few drops of liquid soap)
- $\frac{1}{2}$ cup water
- mixing bowl
- mixing spoon

1 Mix $1\frac{1}{2}$ cups of flour and $\frac{1}{2}$ cup of salt in a mixing bowl.

2 Slowly stir in $\frac{1}{2}$ cup of water and $\frac{1}{4}$ cup of vegetable oil (or a few drops of liquid soap).

3 Squeeze the mixture for about three or four minutes, until it feels like clay. If the mixture breaks apart while you are squeezing it, moisten your hands with water and continue to squeeze.

4 To store unused kitchen clay, place it in an airtight container or a plastic bag. Keep the clay in the refrigerator. If the clay becomes too sticky, squeeze more flour into it.

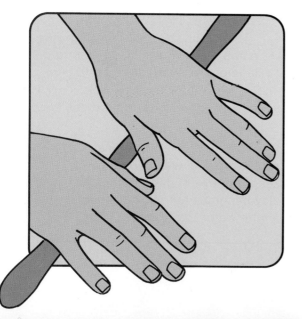

A **ball** of clay can be made from any size lump of clay. To make a ball, roll the clay in a circular motion between your hands.

A **coil** is a ropelike piece of clay. To make a coil, roll the clay back and forth between the flat of your hand and your work surface. Roll from the tips of your fingers to the base of your palm and back again. Roll with both hands from the center to the ends of the coil. Keep doing this until the coil is the size you want.

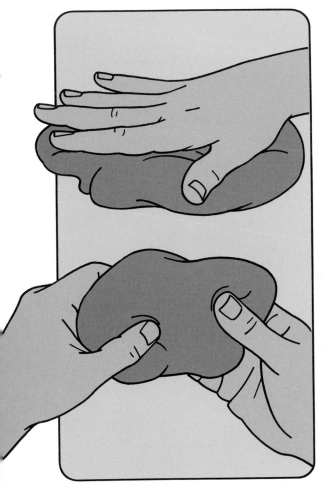

To **flatten** clay, place the clay on your work surface and pat it with the palm of your hand. You can also roll the clay flat with a rolling pin.

To **pinch** clay, press the clay between your thumbs and your first fingers.

To **score** clay, scratch its surface with a toothpick or other pointed tool.

To **texture** clay, draw or carve designs into it with a toothpick or other pointed tool. Or use coins, bottle caps, hairpins, and paper clips to press in designs. You can even stick things into the clay and leave them there. You can use buttons, yarn, paper, cardboard, or any such thing you find around the house.

To **dry** clay, let it stand uncovered for two or three days. The clay will slowly become stiff and hard. But remember, modeling clay will not harden.

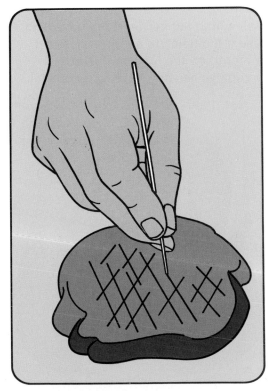

Clay play

Read **Clay** (pages 108-110) before you decide what kind of clay you want to use for this project.

1 Break off a lump of clay about the size of a tennis ball. Roll the clay around between your hands. Did you get a shape like a ball? You will begin most clay projects by making a ball.

2 Now, roll the clay ball back and forth between the flat of your hand and your work surface. Did you get a shape that looks like a piece of rope? This shape is called a coil.

To make a snake, roll one end of the coil a little thinner than the other end. Use a toothpick to scratch eyes and a mouth on the thick end. Draw squiggly lines down the snake's back.

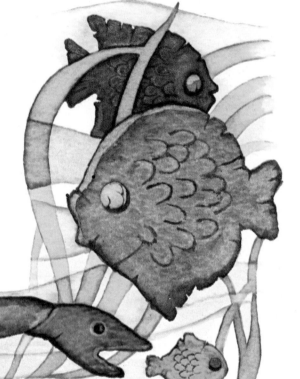

3 Roll the clay back into a ball. Put the clay on your work surface. Pat the clay with the palm of your hand. Did you get a shape like a big cookie?

To make a fish, pinch and pull the edge of the "cookie" to make a mouth, a fin, and a tail. Add a little ball of clay for an eye. To make scales, press a hairpin into the clay.

4 Roll the clay back into a ball.
Pull on two opposite sides of the ball.
Did you pull out two points?

To make a goofy-bird, stick two pencils
into the ball for legs. Add two little
balls of clay for eyes. Use a toothpick
to draw the wings.

5 Roll the clay back into a ball. Poke
your thumbs into the ball. Did you
make a hole?

To make a pinch pot, slowly press the
clay between your thumbs in the hole
and your first fingers on the outside
of the ball (see **pinch**, page 111). Pinch
and press the pot until the sides and
bottom are of even thickness. If you
want, use a toothpick to scratch a
design on your pot.

Thousands of years ago, people made
pots this way. Craftsmen still think
this is a good way to make a pot.

Fruits and vegetables

Read **Clay** (pages 108-111) before you decide what kind of clay you want to use for these projects.

You can create a whole garden of clay fruits and vegetables. Try making pears, bananas, or gourds. If you want to make a clay pot to put your fruits and vegetables in, see page 121.

Let's make an apple!

1 Break off a lump of clay about the size of your fist. Roll the clay into a ball (see **ball**, page 110). With your finger, poke a small hole in the ball.

2 To make a stem, roll a small piece of clay into a coil (see **coil**, page 110). The coil should be about as long and as thick as your little finger.

3 Stick the stem into the hole in the apple. Press the clay around the stem to hold it in place.

4 Break off two small pieces of clay, each about the size of a small marble. Flatten (see **flatten**, page 111) the pieces of clay and shape them into leaves. Stick the leaves to the stem near the apple. Let your apple dry (see **dry**, page 111).

Let's make a carrot!

1 Break off a lump of clay about the size of your fist. Roll the clay into a coil about as long and as fat as a cigar.

Roll one end of the coil a little thinner than the other end. Pat the thin end into a rounded point. With your finger, poke a small hole in the top of the thick end.

2 To make the stems and leaves, roll small pieces of clay into coils. Flatten one end of the coils to form the leaves.

3 Stick the leaf stems into the hole in the carrot. Press the clay around the leaf stems to hold them in place.

4 While the clay is soft, draw lines across the carrot with a toothpick. Let your carrot dry.

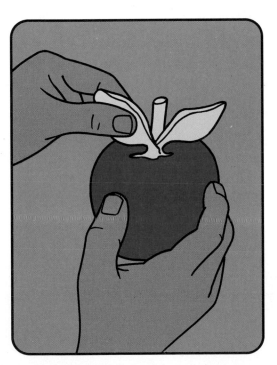

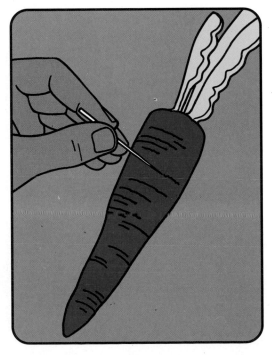

Animal parade

Read **Clay** (pages 108-110) before you decide what kind of clay you want to use for these projects.

Hoofy Horse

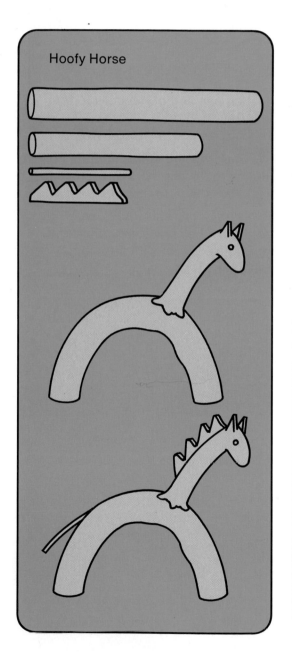

Sleepy Cat

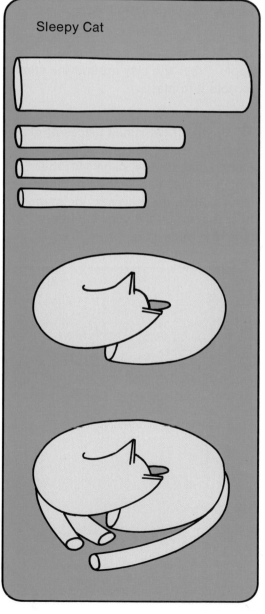

1 To make the cat or horse, break off lumps of clay and roll them into coils (see **coil**, page 110).

To make the duck or dog, break off a lump of clay and roll it into a ball (see **ball**, page 110).

2 Study the pictures. Then, pinch, pull, squeeze, push, poke, pat, and bend the coils and balls to form each animal. Just follow the pictures, step by step.

You can use this method and the one shown in the next project to create a zoo filled with animals.

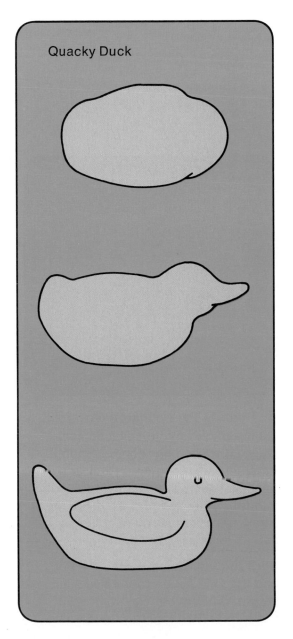

Quacky Duck

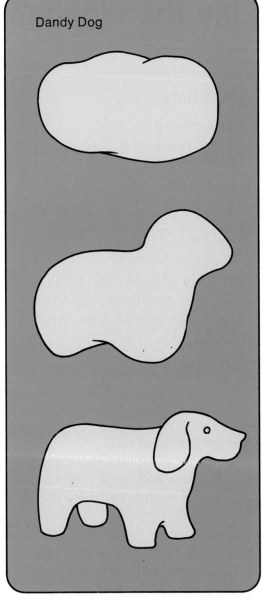

Dandy Dog

Ellie the elephant

Materials

- **cardboard**
- **clay (hardening, modeling, chemical, or kitchen)**
- **scissors**
- **toothpick**

Read **Clay** (pages 108-110) before you decide what kind of clay you want to use for this project.

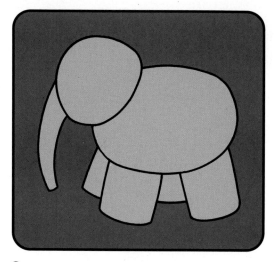

1 To make the elephant's body, break off a lump of clay about the size of a ping-pong ball. Roll the clay into a ball (see **ball,** page 110). Then squeeze and stretch the ball to make it longer than it is wide.

2 For the head, make another ball of clay about the size of a large marble. Stick the head to the body.

3 To make the elephant's legs, roll a lump of clay into a coil (see **coil**, page 110). The coil should be about three times as long and twice as thick as your first finger. Cut the coil into four equal lengths. To make the trunk, roll another coil about as long and as thick as your little finger.

Stick the four fat coils onto the body and the little coil onto the head, as shown. Smooth the clay where the parts are joined together.

4 For the ears, flatten (see **flatten**, page 111) two small lumps of clay. Stick the ears to the head. Make the joint smooth.

5 To make the tail, roll a tiny piece of clay into a coil. Stick it to the elephant's body.

6 Cut two tusks from a piece of cardboard and push them into the clay, one on each side of the trunk.

7 Using a toothpick, poke two little holes in the elephant's head for eyes.

Let dry (see **dry**, page 111).

You can make many other kinds of animals by changing the shapes of the heads, noses, and tails. Try modeling a rhinoceros, a hippopotamus, a lion, or a monkey. Try using yarn, buttons, or pipe cleaners for tails, manes, eyes, arms, and legs.

Coil pot pottery

Materials

- **clay (hardening or chemical)**
- **small dish**
- **toothpick**
- **water**

Read **Clay** (pages 108-110) before you decide what kind of clay you want to use for this project.

1 Break off a lump of clay about the size of a golf ball. To form the bottom part of the pot, flatten (see **flatten**, page 111) the clay until it is about as thick as your first finger.

Push the bottom into the shape you want your pot to be (circles and ovals work best).

2 Break off a lump of clay about the size of a large marble. Roll the clay into a coil (see **coil**, page 110). Make the coil about as thick as your first finger and long enough to go around the bottom part.

3 To start building the sides of the pot, score (see **score**, page 111) one side of the coil and the edge of the bottom part. Moisten the scored edges with water to help them stick. Now, place the coil around the edge of the bottom part so that the scored edges meet. Stick the ends of the coil together.

4 Repeat step 2. Score one side of the coil you just made and the top of the coil already in place.

Moisten the scored edges with water and stick the second coil on top of the first one. Stick the ends of the coil together. Gently push the two coils together so that there are no holes in the side of your pot.

5 Continue rolling, scoring, and sticking on coils until the pot is as tall as you want it to be.

If you want, you can stick one or two handles onto the pot.

Let dry (see **dry**, page 111). You can put flowers or clay fruits into your pot and give it to someone you love.

People projects

Materials

- clay (hardening, modeling, chemical, or kitchen)
- toothpick or other pointed tool

Read **Clay** (pages 108-110) before you decide what kind of clay you want to use for this project.

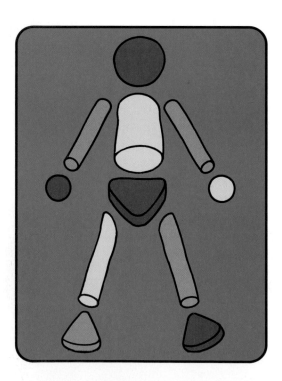

1 For the body, roll a clay lump into a ball (see **ball**, page 110). Stretch it so it is longer than it is wide.

2 For the head, roll another lump of clay into a ball. Stick the head to the body. Smooth the two parts together. To form the neck, gently squeeze the clay where the head joins the body.

3 For the hips, shape a lump of clay to look like a rounded triangle. Stick and smooth the hips to the body.

4 For legs and arms, roll four lumps of clay into coils (see **coil**, page 110).

For feet, stick and smooth two little triangles to the legs. Stick and smooth the legs to the hips.

For hands, stick and smooth two little balls of clay to the arms. Stick and smooth the arms to the body.

5 Give your model eyes, ears, a nose and a mouth, and some hair and clothes. Draw these with a toothpick or make them by adding little pieces of clay. Let dry (see **dry**, page 111).

It's even more fun to make clay people who are doing things. Can you model clay people catching a ball, taking a nap, petting a cat, driving a car, or riding a horse?

Can you model sad people, shy people, happy people?

Can you model what you want to be when you grow up?

Finger mask

Materials

- **clay (hardening)**
- **glass (small)**
- **pan**
- **water**

Read about **hardening clay** (page 108) before you start this project.

1 To make the face part, break off a lump of clay and flatten it (see **flatten**, page 111) until it is about as thick as your first finger.

Using a small glass as you'd use a cookie cutter, cut out one clay circle.

2 Break off two lumps of clay, each about the size of a large marble. Roll two coils (see **coil**, page 110). These coils should be as long as your circle is round.

3 Score (see **score**, page 111) the edge of the circle and the coils. Moisten the scored edges with water. Then stick the two coils to the edge of the circle.

4 For eyes, nose, and mouth, stick small pieces of clay to the circle.

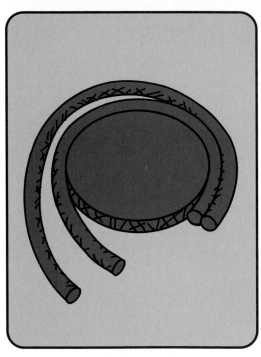

5 To make finger loops, break off a lump of clay about the size of a large marble. Roll the clay into a coil about twice as long and as thick as your first finger. Flatten the coil.

6 Turn in each end of the flattened coil so that you have two circles. The circles should be large enough to fit around your fingers. Score the edges that touch. Then moisten them with water and stick them together.

7 Score the top of the finger loops and the bottom edge of the face. Moisten the scored edges with water and stick them together.

To strengthen the joint between the face and the finger loops, roll a thin coil of clay and gently press it into the joint.

More than a hundred years ago, Inuit used finger masks like this when they acted out stories in dance.

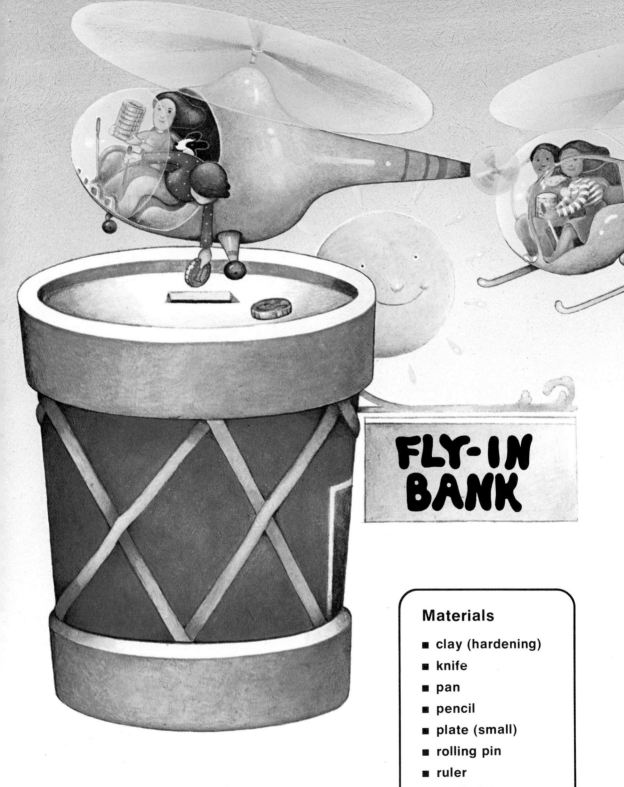

FLY-IN BANK

Drum bank

Materials

- clay (hardening)
- knife
- pan
- pencil
- plate (small)
- rolling pin
- ruler
- toothpick
- water
- wood (two strips of equal thickness)

Read about **hardening clay** (page 108) before you start this project.

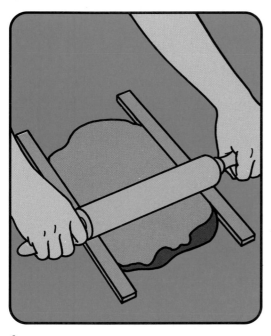

1 Break off a large lump of clay and flatten it (see **flatten**, page 111). Level the flattened clay with a rolling pin. To get an even thickness, place a strip of wood on each side of the clay. Rest the rolling pin on the wooden frame as you roll over the clay. You may have to level more than one lump of clay to make all the pieces.

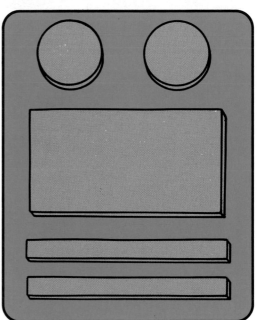

2 Use a knife to cut out the parts of the drum from the leveled clay.

Using a small plate as a guide, cut out two clay circles.

Next, measure and cut out a large slab of clay for the side of the drum bank. This slab should be long enough to go all the way around one of the circles. The wider the strip, the taller the drum bank will be.

Finally, cut out two narrow slabs. Each should be a little longer than the large slab. You will use these slabs in step 8.

(continued on page 128)

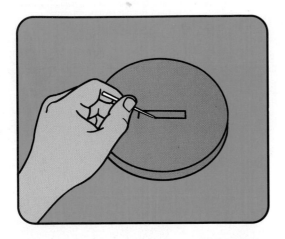

Drum bank

(continued from page 127)

3 With a toothpick, draw a rectangle on one of the clay circles. This will be the coin slot in the top of the drum bank. It should be long enough and wide enough for a large coin. Cut out the rectangle with a knife.

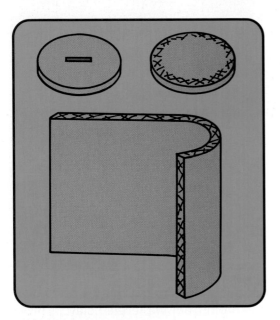

4 Score (see **score**, page 111) the edges of the circles and the four edges of the large clay slab.

5 To stick the side piece to the bottom piece, moisten the scored edges with water. Bend and stick the side onto the bottom piece. Stick the ends together with water. Moisten all the joints with water.

6 Roll a thin coil (see **coil**, page 110) of clay long enough to go around the drum bank. Roll another thin coil that is as long as your drum is tall. Gently press and smooth the coils into the inside and bottom joints.

7 To stick on the top of the drum bank, moisten the scored edge of the top and side pieces with water. Gently press on the top and cover the joint with water.

8 Score one side of each of the two narrow slabs you cut in step 2. Score the side of the drum bank, near the top and bottom. Moisten the scored edges with water. Gently bend the slabs around the drum bank and stick them on.

9 Roll several thin coils of clay. Moisten the coils and the side of the drum with water. Stick the coils on in an X shape, all the way around the drum bank.

10 Let your drum bank dry (see **dry**, page 111). When it is dry, you can paint it with tempera paint (see **tempera paint**, page 66).

On your own

Here are more things you can make with clay.

dollhouse furniture

abacus

diorama

breakfast setting

outer-space figures

pencil holder

Nature Crafts

Nature crafts are collector crafts! All year round, all round the world, nature offers things you can use for craft projects.

On sunshiny spring and summer days, look for sea shells as you walk along sandy beaches, collect leaves on the side of a mountain, or pick some of the flowers blooming in your garden.

Crisp autumn days are perfect for collecting leaves in all their Jack Frost colors. Then is the time to go on a forest adventure, searching for pine cones, acorns, and nuts.

All year long, explore the banks of streams for cattails, marsh grasses, and smooth rocks and stones. And save some seeds from the fruits and vegetables you eat.

Seeds and shells, leaves and flowers, nuts and stones, and pine cones and acorns are only a few of Mother Nature's gifts to you. You'll find many more. By selecting, grouping, shaping, and gluing these natural things, you can make presents for yourself, your parents, and your friends. So turn the page and let Mother Nature be your guide.

Helpful hints

The following information will help you make the projects in this section. If a special skill is needed, the directions will tell you the page on which that skill is explained. For example: "Press the leaves (see **press,** page 135)." If you do not know how to press leaves, you will find directions on page 135.

Seeds of all kinds can be used for seed projects. You can buy some seeds in a grocery store. Others you must save. Make a habit of saving the seeds from apples, oranges, lemons, melons, and other fruits and vegetables. The picture shows some seeds. You will probably think of others.

Seeds used for seed projects must be dry. Most seeds are dry when you buy them. If you are picking seeds or have wet seeds, wash them in cool water. Then spread the seeds on a paper towel and let them dry. This may take one or two days.

To **dye seeds** different colors, put the seeds in a small throwaway container. Mix in drops of food coloring or tempera paint until all the seeds are the color you want. Then, carefully spread the seeds on a paper towel and let them dry for one or two days.

pinto beans

peppercorns

fennel seeds

popcorn

coriander seeds

split peas

black-eyed peas

coffee beans

Lima beans

kidney beans

Use a **leaf press** when collecting leaves. An old magazine or a large book makes a good leaf press. Lay each leaf flat between separate pages This will keep the leaves from curling until you can press them permanently.

To **press leaves or flowers** so they will last a long time, use one of these methods:

Place the leaves or flowers flat between two sheets of newspaper. Always press leaves and flowers separately. If you are pressing flowers, spread out the petals. Leave plenty of space between each leaf or flower. Pile several heavy books on top of the newspaper. Wait at least two weeks for the leaves or flowers to press.

Or, ask a grown-up to help you iron your flowers and leaves. Place the leaves or flowers between two sheets of newspaper. Iron the newspaper with a warm iron.

After you press a leaf or flower, you can **wax** it. Place a sheet of wax paper on top of the leaf or flower and iron first one side and then the other with a warm iron. This will give the leaf or flower more body.

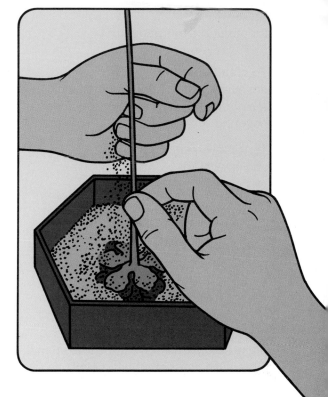

To **dry flowers** so they will keep their shape and last a long time, use one of these methods:

Delicate flowers, such as babies'-breath and snowballs, will dry when tied in bunches and hung upside down in a warm, dry, dark place for two to three weeks. Be sure you remove all the leaves before you hang the flowers.

Sturdy flowers, such as marigolds and zinnias, can be dried in sand. To dry flowers in sand, pour a thin layer of clean, dry sand in the bottom of a shallow box or pan. Place the flowers upside down on the sand. Slowly and carefully cover the flowers with more sand. Keep the uncovered pan in a dry, warm place for one to three weeks.

Store dried flowers in an airtight container in a dark place until you are ready to use them.

(continued on page 136)

Helpful hints

(continued from page 135)

To **clean sea shells,** you must remove any sand, dirt, or tiny animals inside the shell and any hard, crusty material covering the shell.

To remove sand and dirt, wash the shells with soap and water.

To remove any tiny animals living inside, ask a grown-up to help you boil the shells. Place the shells in warm water. Then bring the water to a boil. Let the shells boil about five minutes. Pour off the water and let the shells cool. Use a small crochet hook, nutpick, or bent safety pin to gently twist and pull out the animal. Make sure you remove the entire animal. Otherwise, your shell will smell.

To remove hard, crusty material on the outside, soak the shells in bleach until

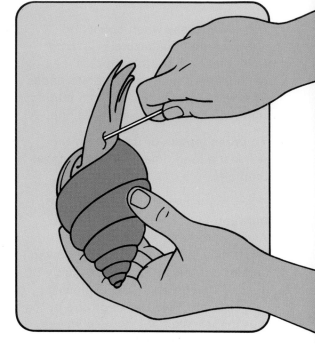

the crust softens. Then carefully chip off the crust with a knife or nutpick.

To **dry sea shells,** gently shake out any water inside. Wipe the shells with a paper towel or a soft cloth.

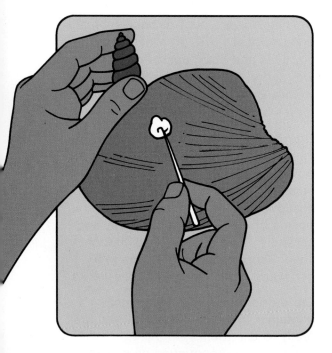

Build **stone or shell sculptures** with glue and cotton. Start at the bottom of your sculpture and work up.

Pour some white glue into a foil pan or jar lid. Use a toothpick to push a tiny piece of cotton or kleenex into the glue.

Put the glued cotton or kleenex between the two stones or shells you want to glue together. Lean the two stones or shells against a box or wall until the glue dries.

Let the glue dry completely before adding another stone or shell. This might take one or more hours.

Mother Nature mobile

Materials

- **flowers or leaves or both**
- **sticks**
- **glue (white)**
- **thread**
- **needle (optional)**

A mobile is a group of hanging objects that move. You can make a pretty mobile from leaves, flowers, and sticks.

1 Collect some leaves, flowers, and sticks. Keep your leaves in a press (see **leaf press,** page 135) while you are collecting them. Press the leaves (see **press,** page 135). Dry the flowers (see **dry,** page 135).

2 Sew or tie the stem of each flower and leaf to a piece of thread. Use a needle, and a thread with a knot at the end, to sew through each stem. Or, just tie the thread around the stems.

3 Hang your leaves and flowers from sticks, as shown. Tie the thread ends around the sticks. Balance each section before you add the next piece.

When your mobile is balanced and looks the way you want it to, dab a little glue on the spots where the threads are fastened. This will keep the threads from slipping.

4 Hang your mobile from the ceiling, in an open doorway, or in some other place where you can watch it dance in the breeze.

You can also make mobiles with sea shells, nut shells, pine cones, acorns, and big seeds.

On your own

Here are more things you
can do with dried plants,
leaves, and sticks.

woven grass mat

**decorated
stationery**

sea-shell scale

bark boats

nature window

flower arrangement

Seed mosaic

A mosaic is a picture made with tiny bits of glass, stone, or other material. The Greeks and Romans made pictures like this to decorate their floors and walls. You can make a mosaic with seeds.

Materials

- cardboard (heavy)
- glue (white)
- pencil or felt-tip pen
- paintbrush
- seeds (see page 134)
- spoon
- varnish

1 Plan a simple picture that has large areas of color. Keep in mind the colors of your seeds. Draw your picture on a piece of heavy cardboard.

2 Glue seeds to the entire design and background. Try not to leave any space between the seeds.

Use a brush, or your finger, to spread glue over a small part of your design. Firmly place the larger seeds on the glue. For smaller seeds, such as poppy seeds, fill a spoon with the seeds and carefully sprinkle them onto the glue. Then spread glue and seeds on another small part of the design. Let dry.

3 When you are finished gluing seeds, brush varnish on the mosaic. This will protect the seeds and will bring out their color.

You can make mosaics from other materials, too. You might want to try colored eggshells or fish-tank gravel. Or, combine seeds with feathers, flowers, and leaves.

On your own

Here are more things you can do with seeds.

map

necklaces

popcorn seedlings

Stone sculpture

Materials

- **cotton**
- **foil pan or jar lid**
- **glue (white)**
- **paintbrush (optional)**
- **rocks and stones**
- **toothpick**
- **varnish (optional)**

Rocks and stones are all different. No two are alike in size, shape, or color. So, you won't be able to make stone sculptures exactly like the ones on the opposite page. But these sculptures will give you an idea of some of the things you can do with rocks and stones.

You can turn a collection of rocks and stones into a delightful group of friends by following these general directions.

1 Wash your rocks and stones to remove any dirt or mud. Let the rocks and stones dry before you begin.

2 Study your rocks and stones. Try to imagine them as parts of animals or people.

For example, flat, triangular shapes could be feet, wings, or ears. Long, round shapes might become arms, legs, or tails. Thick, square, or round shapes make good bodies or bases for other pieces. Use small stones for ears, noses, beaks, mouths, and eyes. Or, paint eyes on tiny white buttons and glue them to the sculpture.

3 Glue the rocks together, stone by stone (see **stone or shell sculptures,** page 136).

4 To decorate your stone sculpture, you can paint it with tempera paint (see **tempera paint,** page 66). Or, you can glue on wire, nuts, pine cones, felt, or yarn. To give your sculpture a shiny look, coat it with varnish.

On your own

Here are more things you
can do with stones.

stone sculptures

flowerpot

rock "aquarium"

Peter the peanut puppet

Materials

- glue (white)
- ice-cream sticks (three)
- needle (darner)
- peanuts (in the shell)
- tempera paint
- thread (heavy)
- yarn

1 For Peter's head and body, string three long peanuts on a long piece of thread. Poke the needle through the shells the long way and pull the thread through. You may have to twist the needle to get it through the shell.

Tie big knots at the top and bottom so the peanuts won't slip off the thread. Leave a long tail of thread above Peter's head.

2 To make hands and arms and legs and feet, string small and long peanuts to Peter's body, as shown. Tie a big knot so the hands and feet won't slip off the string.

3 Paint Peter's face and clothes with tempera paints (see **tempera paint**, page 66). Let the paint dry.

4 For hair, glue on small pieces of yarn. Do not glue over the thread on Peter's head. Let the glue dry.

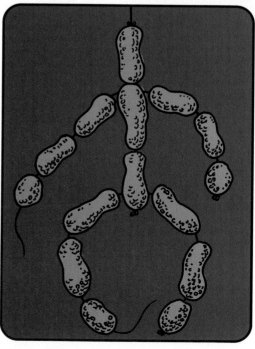

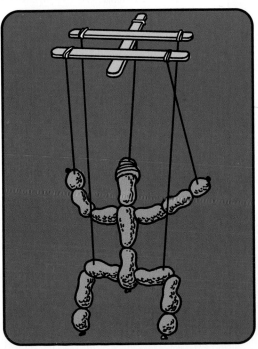

5 Make a control stick by gluing three ice-cream sticks together.

6 Attach control threads to Peter, as shown. Tie a knot at the end of each thread so the peanuts won't slip off. Tie Peter's hand strings to the front crosspiece. Tie his legs to the back crosspiece. Tie the thread on Peter's head to the center control stick.

Dab a little glue on the control stick where the threads are tied. This will keep the threads from slipping off the control stick.

7 To make Peter move, hold the control stick with one hand and pull the control strings with your other hand.

On your own

Here are more things you can do with nuts and cones.

pine-cone animals

perpetual calendar

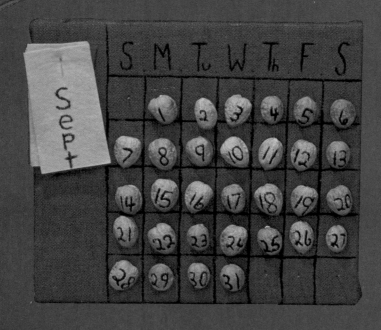

musical instruments

decorated candles

Shell frames

Materials

- **glue (white)**
- **newspaper**
- **paintbrush**
- **unframed mirror**
- **picture hook**
- **sea shells**
- **varnish**

You can find sea shells along the beach. Or, you can buy them in some variety stores, craft shops, pet shops, or import stores.

1 Clean and dry your shells (see **clean and dry sea shells,** page 136).

2 Glue shells around the border of the mirror. Brush glue onto a small part of the border. Firmly place shells onto the glued section. Or, brush glue on one side of a shell. Then firmly place the shell along the border.

Put any cracked and broken shells on first. Glue the prettiest shells on top of these.

Continue gluing shells until you have covered the entire border.

3 When you are finished gluing on shells, varnish the shells. This will protect the shells and bring out their color.

4 Glue a picture hook to the back of the mirror and it is ready to hang up.

You can use shells to decorate all kinds of things. Cover an old picture frame with shells or try making a shell-covered vase from a glass jar, or a treasure chest from a cigar box.

Shell sculpture

Materials

- cotton
- foil pan or jar lid
- glue (white)
- sea shells
- tiny white buttons (optional)
- toothpick
- varnish (optional)

Sea shells grow in many different sizes, shapes, and colors. You can find them along the beach, or buy them. Your shells may not be just like the ones shown on the next two pages, but you can invent sculptures of your own with other kinds of shells.

Here are some general directions for turning a collection of sea shells into amusing pets.

1 Clean and dry your shells (see **clean and dry sea shells,** page 136).

2 Study your shells. Try to imagine them as parts of animals or birds. For example, small flat shells make good feet or ears. Round or cone-shaped shells can become bodies or heads. Large, flat shells are good bases for other shells.

3 Glue the shells together, shell by shell (see **stone or shell sculptures,** page 136).

4 Decorate your shell sculpture with tempera paint (see **tempera paint,** page 66). This is an especially good way to give your pets noses, mouths, and eyes. Or, paint eyes on tiny white buttons and glue them to the sculpture. To give your finished shell sculpture a shiny look, coat it with varnish.

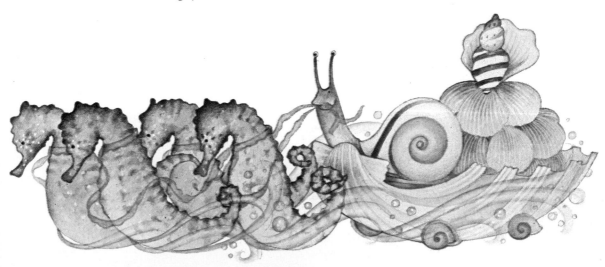

On your own

Here are more things you
can do with shells.

bird feeder

animal sculptures

dresser caddy

dulcimer

wallhanging

Sew and Stitch

Can you paint a picture without paint? Can you turn a sock into a doll? Can you make a snake from a towel? Sound like magic? It is! It's the magic of sew and stitch!

Sewing is easy to learn. And with some practice, it's easy to do. If your first stitches are lumpy and bumpy, don't worry. If you make a mistake, you can pick it out and stitch again. With sewing and stitching, practice does make perfect.

With a needle, some thread, a few scraps of cloth, and a little imagination, you can sew pillows, ponchos, and pictures. And believe it or not, you can even sew a slithery snake.

So stitch your way through the projects in this section. When you're finished, you'll have toys to play with, pillows to pounce on, and maybe even some clothing to wear. It's all part of the magic of sew and stitch.

Helpful hints

The following information will help you make the projects in this section. If a special skill is needed, the directions will tell you the page on which that skill is explained. For example: "Stitch the edges together with the backstitch (see **backstitch,** page 156)." If you do not know how to do the backstitch, you will find directions on page 156.

Thread, needles, scissors, a **ruler** (or tape measure), a **felt-tip pen,** a **thimble,** and **straight pins** are a few of the basic tools needed for sewing.

The threads used most are: sewing thread, embroidery thread, and yarn.

Yarn comes in a roll. It is a thick thread used for decorative stitching. For craft projects, yarn is often used to hold pieces of cloth together.

Embroidery thread comes in packages. It is used for decorative stitching.

Sewing thread comes on a spool. It is used to hold pieces of cloth together.

Selecting the right needle is an important step in sewing. A needle has a hole, or eye, at one end and a point at the other end. There are different kinds of needles.

A **sharp** is a short, thin needle with a small eye. It's used with sewing thread.

A **crewel** is a short needle with a long eye. It's used with embroidery thread.

A **darner** is a long needle with a big eye. It's used with thick thread, such as yarn.

A **tapestry** is a short needle with a big eye. It's also used with thick thread.

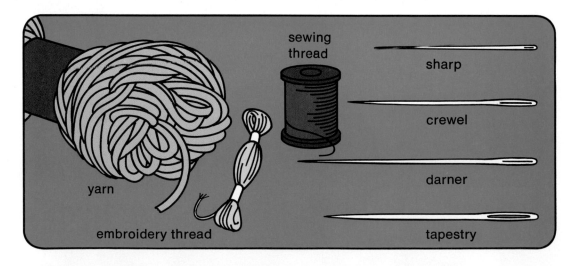

sewing thread

sharp

crewel

darner

tapestry

yarn

embroidery thread

To **thread the needle,** cut off a piece of thread about as long as your arm. Cut it on an angle to make a point. Moisten the cut end and pull it through your fingers. Push it through the eye of the needle and pull it down so the thread won't slip out. Make a small, tight knot at the other end of the thread to keep it from going through the cloth.

To **start a stitch,** push the needle through one side of the cloth and pull it out on the other side. Pull the thread through the cloth until it is stopped by the knot at the end.

To **finish off stitches,** push the needle through to the back of the cloth. Then make two small stitches, one on top of the other. Slide the needle under these two stitches and pull the thread through. Cut off the thread just beyond these stitches.

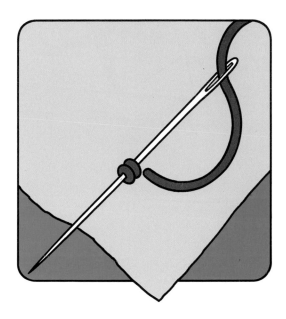

Here are seven basic stitches you should learn how to do. You can practice these stitches on a piece of cloth or paper. Always sew with the needle pointing away from your body.

running stitch

The **running stitch** is a short stitch used to hold pieces of cloth together. Stitches on both sides of the cloth should be the same size and evenly spaced. Weave the needle through the cloth four or five times before you pull the thread through.

(continued on page 156)

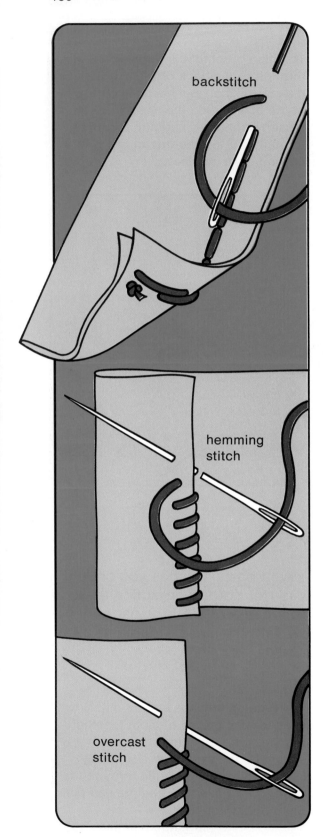

backstitch

hemming
stitch

overcast
stitch

Helpful hints

(continued from page 155)

The **backstitch** is a very strong stitch used to hold pieces of cloth together. Pull the needle and thread through the pieces of cloth, from the back to the front. Move the needle backward about $\frac{1}{2}$ inch (1 cm) from the spot where you pulled the thread through. Now push the needle through to the back of the cloth and pull the needle and thread through. You have made one stitch. Push the needle through to the front of the cloth, $\frac{1}{2}$ inch (1 cm) in front of the stitch you just made. Take the needle back to the end of that stitch. Push the needle in there and pull the needle and thread through to the back of the cloth. Now push the needle through to the front of the cloth, again $\frac{1}{2}$ inch (1 cm) in front of the last stitch you made.

The **hemming stitch** is used to hold down an unfinished edge of folded cloth. Fold down the unfinished fabric edge so the back sides of the cloth are together. With the tip of the needle, pick up a tiny piece of cloth near the unfinished edge. Then pick up a tiny piece of cloth from the unfinished edge of the folded fabric. Pull the needle and thread through both parts of the cloth. It is easier to pick up the cloth if you slant the needle.

The **overcast stitch** is used to keep an edge of cloth from unraveling or to hold pieces of cloth together. Push the needle through to the front of the cloth, just below the edge, and pull the thread through. Then take the thread over the edge to the back of the cloth. Push the needle through to the front again and pull the thread through. Do this stitch over and over until you reach the end of the edge.

The **satin stitch** is used to fill in a design that has been drawn on a piece of cloth. Start at an edge of the shape you want to fill in. Pull the needle and thread through to the front of the cloth. Stitch from one edge to the opposite edge until the shape is filled in. Don't pull the thread too tight or the cloth will bunch up.

The **chain stitch** is used to decorate a piece of cloth. Push the needle through, from the back to the front of the cloth. Then pull the thread through. Now push the needle in next to the spot where the thread comes out. Pull the thread through to the back of the cloth until there is a small loop left on the front of the cloth. Hold the loop down with your thumb and push the needle through to the front of the cloth, inside the loop. Push the needle in beside the spot where you pulled the thread through. Pull the thread through to the back of the cloth, making another small loop inside the first loop.

Keep making loops inside of loops until you have a long chain. To finish off the chain, make a small stitch over the last loop.

The **lazy daisy stitch** is made somewhat like the chain stitch. Make a loop, as you did in the chain stitch. Hold the loop down with your thumb. Now push the needle back through the loop and pull the thread through to the front of the cloth. Push the needle in again, just outside the loop. Pull the thread through to the back of the cloth. Poke the needle through to the front of the cloth wherever you want the next loop. Repeat this until you finish the daisy design.

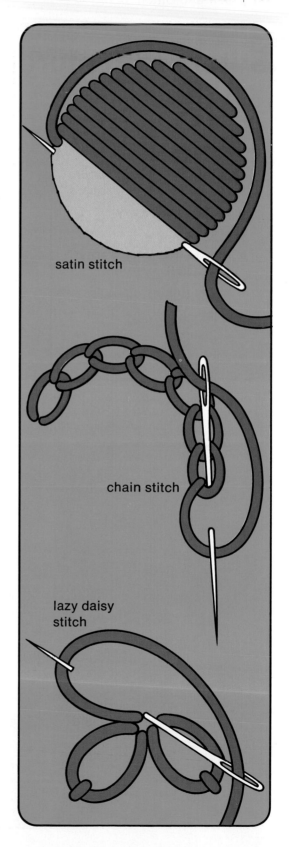

satin stitch

chain stitch

lazy daisy stitch

Stitchery picture

Materials

- **burlap or canvas, about 12 inches (30 cm) square**
- **cardboard (heavy)**
- **crayon**
- **needle (tapestry, darner, or crewel)**
- **paper (plain)**
- **ruler**
- **scissors**
- **yarn (several colors)**

1 Plan and draw a design or picture on a piece of paper. You can make up your own design or get ideas from pictures in magazines or books.

2 Use a crayon to copy your design on burlap or canvas. Now look at the different stitches shown in **Helpful hints,** pages 154–157. Use some or all of these stitches to outline and fill in your design. Use as many different colors of yarn as you like. Don't forget to finish off all your sewing (see **finish off,** page 155).

3 If you want a fringe, pull a few threads from each edge of the burlap.

Hang your picture on a wall or use it as a place mat.

Stitched belt

Materials

- cloth scraps
- felt or heavy cotton,
  2 inches (5 cm) wide and long
  enough to go around your waist
- embroidery thread
- felt-tip pen
- needle (tapestry, darner,
  or crewel)
- scissors
- straight pins
- yarn

1 Plan the design for your belt
on a piece of plain paper. Now draw
the shapes in your design on pieces
of cloth. Cut out these cloth shapes.

2 Pin the cloth shapes to the belt.
Using embroidery thread, stitch the
shapes to the belt with the overcast
stitch (see **overcast stitch,** page 156).
Finish off your sewing (see **finish
off,** page 155).

3 Draw other shapes on the belt with
a felt-tip pen. Outline or fill in
these shapes with the chain stitch
(see **chain stitch,** page 157) and the
satin stitch (see **satin stitch,** page
157). Finish off your stitches.

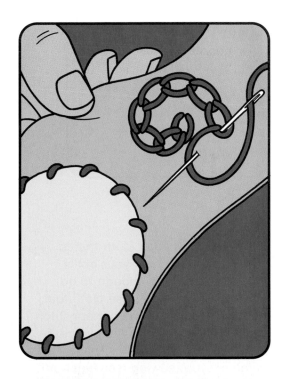

4 To make ties for the belt, cut
three pieces of yarn 12 inches (30 cm)
long. Now cut these three pieces
in half.

5 Place three of the pieces of yarn
together so that the ends meet. Tie a
knot at both ends. Now stitch a
knotted end of the yarn to one end of
the belt. Stitch above and below the
knot. Finish off your stitches. Repeat
step 5 for the other tie.

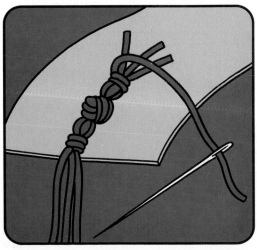

Doll's poncho

Materials

- cloth
- cloth scraps
- embroidery thread
- felt-tip pen
- needle (crewel, darner, or tapestry)
- ruler
- scissors
- straight pins
- yarn

1 Choose a piece of cloth that is wide enough to cover your doll's shoulders and long enough to go below its waist. If you use cloth that unravels easily, such as burlap, stitch around the edges with the overcast stitch (see **overcast stitch,** page 156). Finish off your sewing (see **finish off,** page 155).

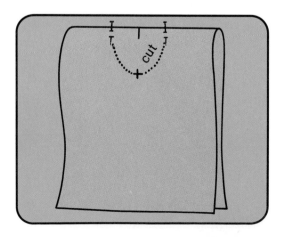

2 Fold the cloth in half so that the short ends meet evenly. Now find the center of the folded edge and make a mark there with a felt-tip pen.

Measure an equal distance from each side of the center mark. Put pins at these two points. The distance between the pins must be a little wider than your doll's head.

Measure the distance between the pins. Now measure the same distance down from the center mark. Make a mark here. Using this mark and the pins as guides, draw a U-shaped or V-shaped neck opening. Keep the cloth folded and carefully cut out the neck opening.

3 Stitch around the edges of the neck opening with the overcast stitch. Finish off your sewing. Now decorate the poncho with different kinds of stitches, or use the overcast stitch to sew on shapes cut from cloth.

4 Use four short pieces of yarn to make ties for the poncho. All the pieces should be the same length. Make a knot at both ends of each piece of yarn. Sew an end of each piece of yarn to the poncho, as shown. Place the poncho over your doll's head. Tie the pieces of yarn together to fasten the poncho.

If you have a large piece of cloth, try making a poncho for yourself.

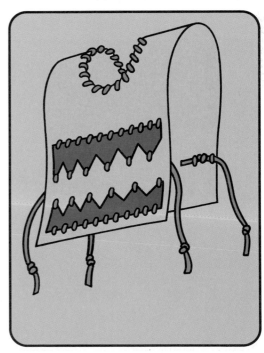

Fringed pillow

Materials

- **burlap or canvas,
  12 inches (30 cm) wide
  and 24 inches (60 cm) long**
- **felt, 8 inches (20 cm) square**
- **felt-tip pen**
- **needle (tapestry, darner,
  or crewel)**
- **scissors**
- **straight pins**
- **stuffing (old, cut-up socks,
  stockings, or rags)**
- **yarn**

1 Fold the burlap in half so that the short edges meet evenly. Cut the burlap in half along the fold line to make two squares.

2 Draw a large circle on the felt. Cut out the circle and draw a face on it with a felt-tip pen.

Use the chain stitch (see **chain stitch,** page 157) to outline the eyes, nose, and mouth. Finish off your sewing (see **finish off,** page 155).

3 Now pin the face to the center of one of the burlap squares. Stitch the edges to the burlap with the overcast stitch (see **overcast stitch,** page 156). Be sure to finish off your sewing.

4 Pin the burlap squares together on all four sides. Place the pins about 1 inch (2 cm) from the edges. Use the backstitch (see **backstitch,** page 156) to sew *three* of the sides together. Stitch just below the pins. Finish off your sewing.

5 Take out the pins and push stuffing into the pillow through the open side. Make the pillow nice and fat. Now stitch the open side closed with the backstitch. Finish off your sewing.

6 To fringe the pillow, pull five or six threads out of each edge of the burlap. Do not pull the threads too close to the stitches or the stuffing may come out.

Use your pillow to decorate your bed or give it to a friend as a gift.

Sock doll

Materials

- **buttons (two)**
- **cardboard (heavy)**
- **dry beans or pebbles**
- **felt**
- **glue (white)**
- **needle (tapestry, darner, or crewel)**
- **paper**
- **ribbon**
- **scissors**
- **sock (old)**
- **straight pins**
- **stuffing (old, cut-up rags or paper toweling)**
- **yarn**

1 Cut off an old sock just above the heel. Push stuffing into the sock. To add weight, put a handful of beans or pebbles into the sock last.

2 Pull the edges of the sock together. Tuck them under and fold one side over the other. Pin the fold to the stuffed part of the sock. Use the hemming stitch (see **hemming stitch, page 156**) to sew it down. Finish off your sewing (see **finish off, page 155**).

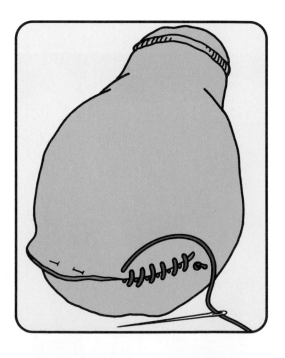

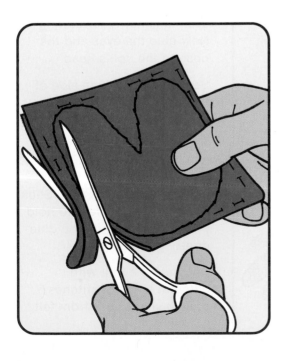

3 To form the doll's neck, gently squeeze the sock just above the toe. Tie a ribbon around the neck to keep the head separated from the body.

4 On a piece of heavy cardboard, draw a pattern for the feet. Cut out the feet and trace them on a piece of doubled felt. Now pin the felt together and cut around the feet, through both pieces of felt.

5 Glue one piece of felt to the top and the other piece to the bottom of the cardboard pattern.

(continued on page 168)

Sock doll

(continued from page 167)

6 Draw patterns for a nose, an eye, and an arm on a piece of paper. Pin the patterns for the eye and the arm on a piece of doubled felt. Cut around the patterns, through both pieces of felt to get two eyes and two arms.

7 Pin the pattern for the nose to a single piece of felt. Cut out the nose. For decoration, use the overcast stitch (see **overcast stitch, page 156**) to stitch with yarn around the edges of the nose. Finish off your sewing.

8 Use yarn to sew a button to the center of each cloth eye. Finish off your sewing. Now glue the eyes and the nose to the doll's head.

Sew an arm to each side of the doll's body with the overcast stitch. Finish off your sewing.

9 Now glue the feet to the bottom of the sock doll. Stick pins through the feet to hold them in place while the glue dries.

Decorate the doll with different kinds of stitches or with shapes cut from felt.

Slither the snake

Materials

- bath towel or dish towel
- felt-tip pen
- felt scraps
- needle (tapestry, darner, or crewel)
- ruler
- scissors
- straight pins
- stuffing (old, cut-up socks, stockings, or rags)
- yarn

1 Measure 10 inches (25 cm) in from one of the long edges of the towel. Make a mark there. Do this in several places. Using the marks as a guide, draw a straight line on the towel. Cut along the line. You will use this strip of towel for Slither's body.

2 Measure $2\frac{1}{2}$ inches (6 cm) in from one of the long edges of Slither's body. Make marks and draw a line as you did in step 1.

With yarn, make a row of chain stitches (see **chain stitch,** page 157) along the line you just drew. Finish off your sewing (see **finish off,** page 155).

(continued on page 170)

Slither the snake

(continued from page 169)

3 Fold the strip in half, the long way, with the chain stitches on the inside. Pin the long edges and one short end. Place the pins about $\frac{1}{2}$ inch (1 cm) from the edges.

With the backstitch (see **backstitch, page 156**), stitch the pinned edges together just below the pins. Finish off your sewing.

Take out the pins and turn Slither inside out, through the open end.

4 Push stuffing in through the open end. You may have to use a ruler or a long stick to help push the stuffing in. Make Slither nice and fat.

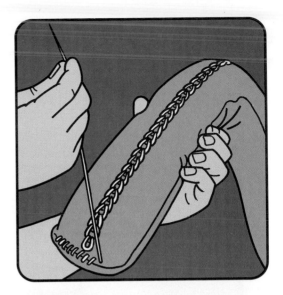

5 Fold the edges of the open end under about $\frac{1}{2}$ inch (1 cm) and pin them together. Using yarn, stitch the opening closed with the overcast stitch (see **overcast stitch,** page 156). Finish off your sewing. This end is Slither's head.

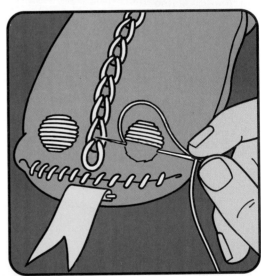

6 Cut out a shape for Slither's tongue from a piece of felt. Sew the tongue on just below the overcast stitching. Draw an eye on each side of the row of chain stitches. Use the satin stitch (see **satin stitch,** page 157) to fill in the eyes with yarn. Slither the snake is ready to live in your room.

On your own

Here are more things you
can make with needle
and thread.

snail pillow

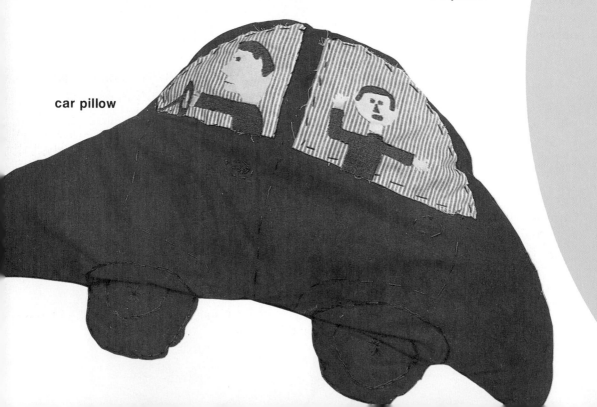

car pillow

curtain and vest

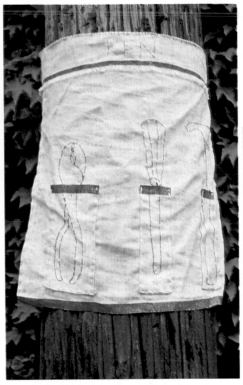

tool apron

string-bean pillow

wallhanging

Hook, Weave, Knot, and Braid

It's raining, it's pouring, and Bob and Sue are weaving yarn bags!

Janie's going on a long trip. On the way, she's making an octopus to keep her company.

Bill's not playing ball. He's weaving a tapestry for his mom's birthday.

Bob, Sue, Janie, and Bill know that hook, weave, knot, and braid projects are good anytime, anyplace, stop-and-start projects.

Most hook, weave, knot, and braid projects are simple to make, but they do take time. Some take several days or weeks to complete. But when they're finished, these projects are pretty to look at, fun to play with, and will last much longer than it took to make them.

You can make hundreds of things by hooking, weaving, knotting, and braiding. The projects in this section are only a beginning. When you've made them, you'll want to create hook, weave, knot, and braid projects of your own.

Helpful hints

The following information will help you make the projects in this section. If a special skill is needed, the directions will tell you the page on which that skill is explained. For example: "Hook the design on the burlap (see **hooked project,** page 177)." If you do not know how to hook, you will find directions on page 177.

Here are directions for some basic hooks, weaves, knots, and braids. Once you can do these, you'll be able to create hook, weave, knot, and braid patterns of your own.

Hooking

A **hooked project** has little loops or pieces of yarn sticking up from a burlap backing.

A **crochet hook** is used to hook loops of yarn into a burlap backing. This tool is a steel or plastic hook. It comes in various sizes. Size G, or 5, or larger, works best for hooking in burlap.

A **frame** is used to stretch and hold burlap backing while you work on hooked projects. For small projects, use an embroidery hoop. For larger projects, use a picture frame or make a cardboard frame.

Before you make a frame, decide how large you want to make the project area. The project area is the open space within the edges of the frame.

frame

crochet hook

1 To make a cardboard frame, measure and cut four cardboard strips. Each strip should be about 3 inches (8 cm) wide and about 6 inches (15 cm) longer than the project area. Staple the cardboard strips so they form a frame.

2 To use the frame, staple the backing to one edge of the frame. Then stretch the backing tight and staple it to the other edges of the frame.

To start a **hooked project,** use a pencil to draw a design on a piece of burlap. Leave a 2-inch (5-cm) border around the design.

1 Stretch the burlap over a frame. Make sure the design is centered in the project area. Tack or staple the burlap to the frame.

2 Hook the outline of the design first. Hold the yarn underneath the burlap. Poke the crochet hook through the burlap from the top to the bottom. Hook the yarn over the crochet hook. Pull a little loop through to the top of the burlap. Make another loop next to the first one.

3 Carefully pull the end of the yarn from the first loop to the top. Push the end through the second loop and pull the loop tight. Cut the end even with the loop.

4 Now, use the crochet hook to make as many loops as you need to fill in your project. Try to make the loops about $\frac{1}{4}$ inch (6 mm) high.

5 When you come to the end of your yarn, or when you are finished hooking, pull the end of the yarn from the last loop to the top. Push the end through what is now the last loop and pull it tight. Cut the end even with the loops.

6 Finish the project by folding the border under and stitching it down with the hemming stitch (see **hemming stitch,** page 156).

You can create interesting textures in your hooked projects by **sculpturing** and **shearing.** To sculpture, make some of the loops high and others low. To shear, make high loops. When you are finished hooking, cut the loops to different lengths.

(continued on page 178)

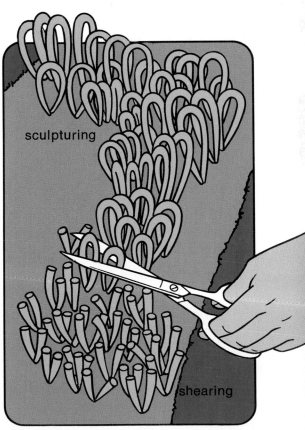

sculpturing

shearing

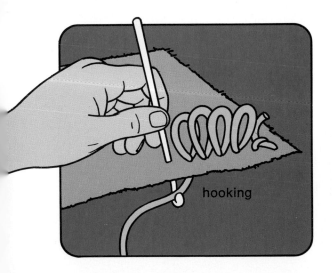

hooking

Helpful hints

(continued from page 177)

Weaving

In **weaving,** threads (or strips of material) are passed over and under each other to make a piece of cloth or to form a design. The threads that go up and down are called the warp. Those that go across are called the weft, or woof. The weft is always woven over and under the warp.

Most weaving is done on a loom. The warp threads are wrapped around the loom. Blunt needles and stick needles threaded with yarn are used to weave the weft over and under the warp.

A **blunt needle** looks like a big sewing needle without a sharp point. It is used to weave thread in narrow places. You can buy one called a tapestry needle or a stole weaving needle.

A **stick needle** is used to hold yarn as you weave. You can make a stick needle from an ice-cream stick or a stiff piece of cardboard. When weaving, thread the stick needle with about 3 feet (1 m) of yarn.

To make a wooden stick needle, use an ice-cream stick. Punch a hole in one end with a hammer and a small nail.

To make a cardboard stick needle, use a piece of stiff cardboard about 1 inch (2.5 cm) wide and 5 inches (12.5 cm) long. Cut a point at one end and punch a hole in the other end.

A **beater** is used to push woven threads together tightly. You can use a fork or a wide-toothed comb to beat your weaving.

A **loom** is used to hold threads being woven into cloth. You can make looms in many different shapes. Your weaving will take the shape of the loom. You can make a simple loom out of cardboard. Or, make a stronger one out of wood.

1 To make a cardboard loom, cut a piece of cardboard the size you want your loom. Measure in about $\frac{1}{2}$ inch (13 mm) from the top and bottom of the cardboard and draw lines.

2 Place a ruler along the lines and make a mark every $\frac{1}{4}$ inch (6 mm). Use a ruler to draw slanted lines from the marks to the edge of the cardboard.

3 Cut along the slanted lines, stopping at the straight line. When you are finished, you will have notches that look like rows of teeth along the top and bottom of the loom.

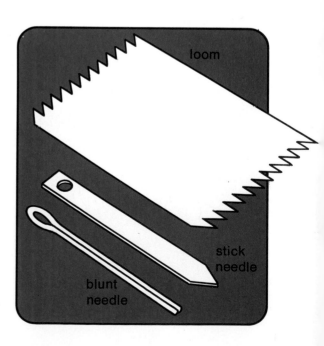

loom

stick needle

blunt needle

There are many weaving patterns, all fun to do. You can even make a special knot to give your weaving a shaggy look. The pictures show you how to start and finish off yarn ends, do two basic weaves, and make a **Ghiordes knot.**

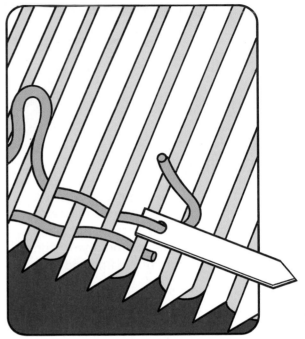

plain weave

basket weave

Start your weaving at the bottom center of the loom. Weave toward one edge. Loop the thread around the last warp strand and then weave back toward the other edge.

Finish off your weaving when you reach the end of a piece of yarn, when you finish a color, or when you complete a project. To finish off, weave the yarn end back into the weaving to hold the end in place.

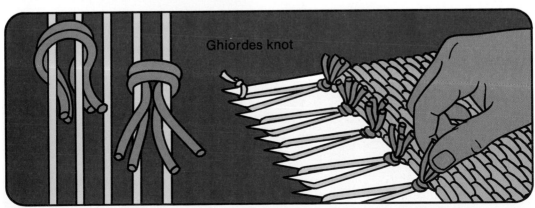

Ghiordes knot

(continued on page 180)

Helpful hints

(continued from page 179)

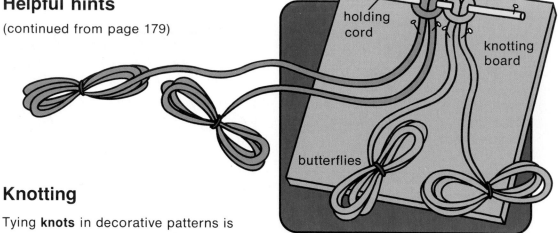

Knotting

Tying **knots** in decorative patterns is called macramé. For most macramé projects you will need several lengths of cord, each measuring about eight times the length of the finished project.

The pictures show you how to make a knotting board, make butterflies, start a project, and tie a **square knot.**

Butterflies make the long cord ends easy to handle. To butterfly a cord end, wrap the cord around your hand until about 12 inches (30 cm) of cord is left near the beginning knot. Slide the cord off your hand and put a rubber band around the butterfly.

A **knotting board** holds the cords as you tie the knots. Use a block of Styrofoam or a piece of corrugated cardboard as a knotting board. Pin the cords to the board, as shown.

A **lark's head** or **grouped overhand knot** starts the macramé. To begin, fold each cord in half. Use the lark's head knot to attach the folded cords to a holding cord, or tie the folded cords in a grouped overhand knot, as shown.

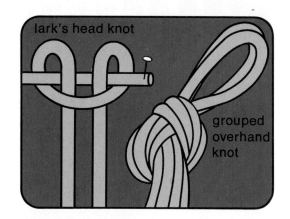

Braiding

A **braid** is a band formed by weaving three or more threads together. You can sew braids together to make belts, bracelets, place mats, and rugs.

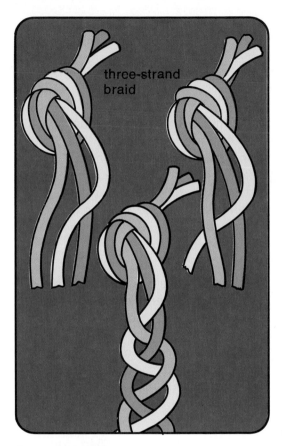

three-strand braid

1 A **three-strand braid** is started by tying three strands of yarn or string in a knot at one end.

2 Bring the right strand over the middle strand. Then bring the left strand over the middle one, and so on.

3 Continue this way, weaving the outside strands over the middle strand. Make a knot at the end when you are finished. If you want to make a fatter braid, use more strands. Divide the strands into three groups.

1 A **four-strand (or more) braid** is started by tying the strands to a pencil.

2 Braid from the right. Pass the strand at the right over and under the other strands. Do the same with the strand that is now at the right. Continue this way until finished.

3 When you are finished braiding, slip the braid off the pencil and knot or sew the loose ends together.

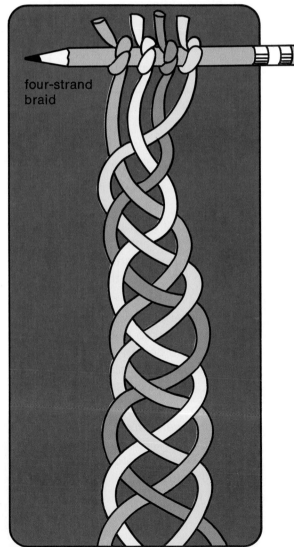

four-strand braid

Burlap wallhanging

Materials

- **blunt needle**
- **burlap**
- **cardboard or wood strip**
- **crochet hook**
- **frame**
- **glue (white)**
- **pencil**
- **scissors**
- **yarn (several colors)**

1 Cut a big piece of burlap the size you want your wallhanging to be.

2 Use a pencil to draw a simple design near the center of the burlap. Your design should be about one-fourth the size of the burlap.

3 Stretch the design part of the burlap over a frame (see **frame**, page 176). Hook the design (see **hooked project**, page 177).

4 At the bottom, make a fringe by pulling out twenty-five or more rows of burlap threads. Braid the fringe (see **three-strand braid**, page 181). Use the threads you pulled out to tie the ends of the braids.

5 At the top, fold about $\frac{1}{2}$ inch (15 mm) of burlap to the back. With a blunt needle threaded with yarn, weave a row of running stitches through the doubled burlap (see **running stitch**, page 155). Leave about 12 inches (30 cm) of yarn at each end of the row of stitches.

6 Above and below your hooked design, pull out and weave rows of burlap thread. Tie groups of up and down threads together. Try twisting the groups of thread and weaving yarn through them. Try weaving yarn between the threads (see **weaving**, page 178).

7 To hang your wallhanging, you will need a strip of stiff cardboard or wood as wide as the burlap. Glue the strip to the back of the wallhanging at the top. Tie the loose ends of yarn from step 5. Hang up your wallhanging.

You can make place mats and seat covers by hooking, weaving, and stitching in burlap. You can hook a vest for yourself by tracing and cutting out the outline of an old jacket or sweater on a piece of doubled burlap.

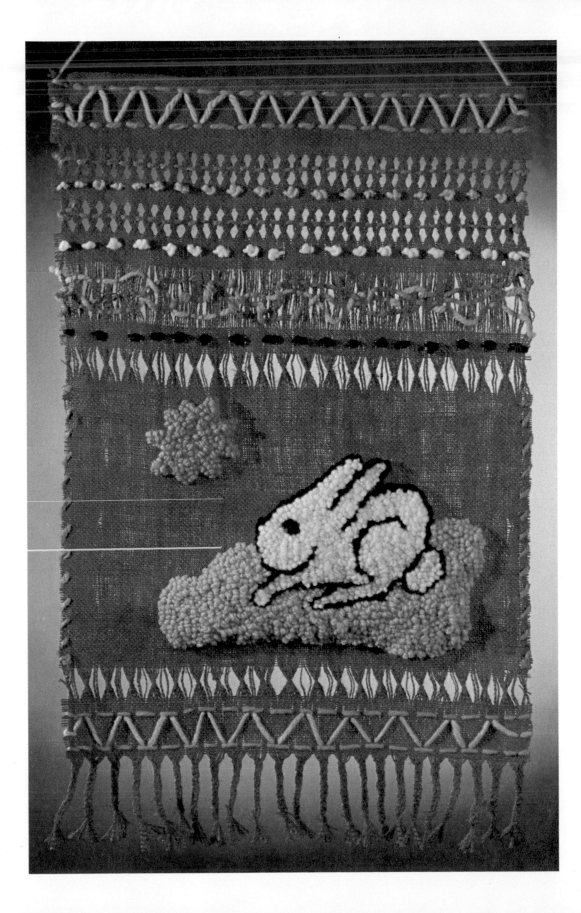

Lanyard lacings

Materials

- **flat plastic lacing (two colors, 3 yards [2.7 m] of each color)**
- **snap hook**
- **scissors**
- **string**

A lanyard is a braided cord or rope. You can buy the materials for this project in a craft shop.

1 Tie a piece of string to the snap end of your snap hook. Now tie the string to a doorknob or chair. This will make it easier for you to braid your lanyard.

2 Push the laces through the snap hook and fold them in half so you have four strands. Arrange the strands as shown.

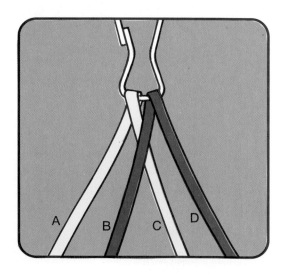

3 Fold strand D under C and B, and then over strand B, as shown. Now fold strand A under B and D, and then over strand D, as shown. Keep the lacing flat as you braid.

Continue braiding this way. Fold the right-hand outside strand under two strands and back over one. Then fold the left-hand outside strand under two strands and back over one. Always work with the **highest outside** strand.

Braid until the cord is long enough to go around your neck and hang down your chest, as shown.

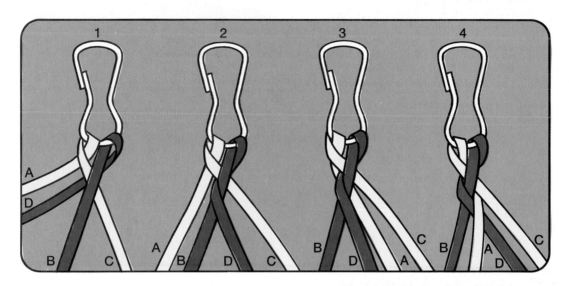

4 When the cord is the length you want, place the hook end of the cord between the lacings, as shown.

Continue to braid around the cord. Do not count the cord as a lace. Make this part of the braid about 1 inch (2.5 cm) long and loose enough for the hook-end cord to slide up and down through the braiding.

5 When you are finished braiding, tie each pair of opposite-color laces once. Cut off the ends, leaving tails about 1 inch (2.5 cm) long.

You can use your lanyard to hold a whistle, a pendant, or a key. You can make a long lanyard and use it as a belt or a leash for your pet. A short lanyard makes a sturdy key chain.

Octavius octopus

> **Materials**
>
> - **blunt needle**
> - **scissors**
> - **Styrofoam or rubber ball (or tightly crumpled newspaper)**
> - **yarn (two colors)**

1 Cut off 36 strands of yarn, each measuring three times as long as your ball is round. You will use these strands to cover the ball.

2 Lay the strands of yarn on your work surface so the ends are even. With a piece of yarn, tie the strands together at the middle.

3 To begin the head and legs, place the ball on top of the knot. Arrange the strands of yarn around the ball.

4 Use a piece of yarn to tie the strands in a bunch, as shown.

5 To make Octavius' legs, divide the loose strands of yarn into eight bunches. Braid each bunch (see **three-strand braid,** page 181). You do not need to tie a knot at the beginning or end of a braid. Tie the ends with a piece of yarn.

6 For hair, cut strands of yarn about 3 inches (8 cm) long. Weave them in a Ghiordes knot around the top of Octavius' head (see **Ghiordes knot,** page 179).

7 With a blunt needle, weave yarn around Octavius' body (see **plain weave,** page 179). When you reach the end of the yarn, finish off and start weaving with a new piece (see **start** and **finish off,** page 179).

8 To make the eyes and nose, use a blunt needle to weave yarn in a satin stitch (see **satin stitch,** page 157). For the mouth, weave a chain stitch (see **chain stitch,** page 157).

If you want, you can braid a string tie for Octavius.

Weave a bag

Read **weaving** (pages 178-179) before you begin this project.

1 Cut a piece of cardboard the size you want your bag to be. Leave an extra $\frac{1}{2}$ inch (13 mm) along the edge that will be the top of the bag.

Use the cardboard to make a notched loom (see **loom**, page 178). Make notches along the **top edge only**.

2 For the warp, wind yarn around the loom, as shown. Tie the yarn around the first notch at the left. Then loop the yarn around the notches, passing the yarn around the loom from top to bottom and from front to back. You should loop the yarn twice around each notch, once from the front and once from the back. You should have warp yarns on both the front and back sides of the loom. When you get to the right-hand edge of the loom, tie the yarn around the last notch.

Materials

- blunt needle
- cardboard (stiff)
- fork or comb
- pencil
- ruler
- scissors
- stick needle
- yarn

3 Use the basket weave (see **basket weave**, page 179) to make the bag. Begin weaving at the middle of the edge opposite the notches (see **start** and **finish off**, page 179). Pull the weft yarns through the warp with a stick needle (see **stick needle,** page 178). When you reach the last warp strand, turn the loom over and continue weaving on the other side. Keep weaving around and around. Beat the threads together as you weave (see **beater**, page 178).

Finish off your weaving about 1 inch (2.5 cm) from the top of the bag.

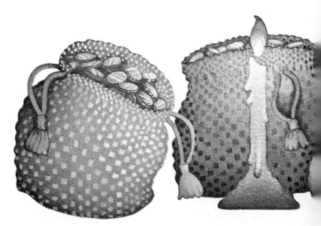

4 For handles, make two braids (see **three-strand braid,** page 181). Cut the yarn for each strand at least four times as long as the top of your bag.

Weave each braid in a basket weave around the front and back of the bag. Tie together the ends of each braid.

5 Use a blunt needle to finish the bag with a plain weave (see **plain weave,** page 179). Whenever you weave a bag, you must finish off the top with a plain weave to keep the weaving from coming apart.

6 Carefully unhook each loop from around the notches. Loop the knotted ends around the last row of weaving, as shown. Tuck in the ends.

You can use your bag to hold marbles or toys. Or, you can use the bag as a coin bag or purse.

Knots 'n pots macramé

Read **knotting** (page 180) before you begin this project.

Materials

- **corrugated cardboard or Styrofoam**
- **curtain ring (optional)**
- **jute**
- **pins or thumbtacks**
- **scissors**
- **tin can, jar, or flowerpot**

1 Cut six pieces of cord. For this project, each cord should be about five times as long as the distance you want your pot to hang down. (The rule that cords should measure eight times the finished length does not apply here because there are only a few knots.)

2 Fold the cords in half so you have twelve strands. Tie the folded cords together in a grouped overhand knot, or hitch them to a curtain ring with lark's head knots (see **lark's head** or **grouped overhand knots,** page 180).

3 Divide the cords into three groups of four cords each.

4 Pin one group of cords to a knotting board (see **knotting board,** page 180).

Tie two square knots (see **square knot,** page 180) about $\frac{1}{2}$ inch (13 mm) below the beginning knots. Leave the knots loose enough so you can see the design. Tie two knots like this for each group of cords.

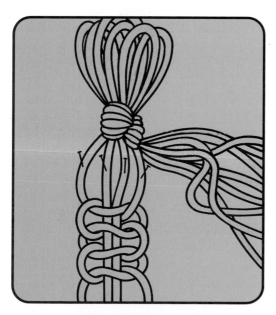

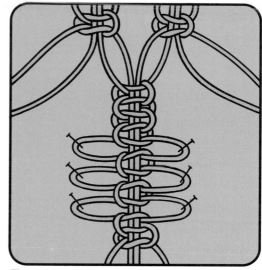

5 Take two cords from each group to make three new groups of four cords each. Leave a 2-inch (5-cm) space. Tie two square knots in each new group. Next, tie three tight square knots with loops, as shown. Put pins in the board to hold the loops evenly. Then tie one square knot.

6 Take two cords from each group to make three new groups of four. Leave a 2-inch (5-cm) space. Tie three square knots in each new group. Leave a 2-inch (5-cm) space. Tie three more square knots.

7 Tie all the cords together in a grouped overhand knot near the ends.

8 Place a tin can, jar, or flowerpot filled with flowers or plants in your macramé hanger. Hang the pot from a hook, and enjoy your little garden hanging in the air.

You can make macramé projects to hang up your toys and macramé projects to wear. By making the knots closer together, you can make a belt.

Tapestry weaving

Materials

- **blunt needle**
- **cardboard (stiff)**
- **crayons or felt-tip pens**
- **fork or comb**
- **paper (blank)**
- **scissors**
- **stick needles (three or more)**
- **string**
- **yarn (two or more colors)**

A tapestry is a woven picture. Read **weaving** (page 178) before you begin this project.

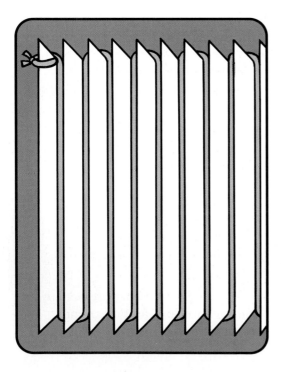

1 Make a loom (see **loom,** page 178).

2 Cut a piece of paper the same size as your loom. Draw a line around the paper, leaving a 1-inch (2.5-cm) border.

Inside the border, draw and color the design or picture you want to weave. For your first tapestry, it is best to start with a two-color design—one color for the background and another color for the design.

3 For the warp, tie and wind string on the loom as shown.

4 Tape your drawing under the warp strings. Use it as a guide.

5 Begin weaving at the bottom. Weave eight or more rows of background in a plain weave (see **plain weave,** page 179). Beat the threads together as you weave (see **beater,** page 178).

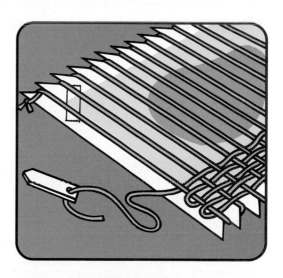

Mix different weave patterns to create interesting textures. For the picture, use a plain or basket weave. Always use the plain weave for the background.

6 Use a different stick needle (see **stick needle,** page 178) for each color yarn in the picture. Use two needles for the background, one to weave the right-hand side of the background and one to weave the left-hand side.

Weave your design row by row. Link the background color with the picture color, as shown. Always link one background row with each picture row. Beat the threads as you weave.

7 To finish off your tapestry at the top, weave eight or more rows of background in a plain weave.

When you are finished weaving, carefully unhook each loop from around the notches. Loop the knotted ends around the last row of weaving, as shown. Tuck in the ends.

In the Middle Ages, tapestries were used as wall hangings in castles. You can use your tapestry as a wall hanging, pillow cover, place mat, or seat cover. You can also weave a bag (see page 188) with a tapestry design.

On your own

Here are more things you can make with yarn, string, and rope.

braided loops

woven-and-hooked pillow

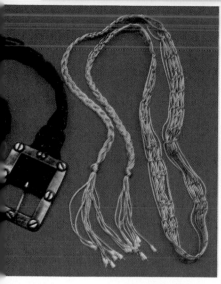

macramé belts

woven-and-braided doll

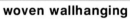

woven wallhanging

tapestry

Working with Wood

Wood is all around you! You walk on wooden floors and open wooden doors. Most window frames are made of wood. And the chair you're sitting on probably has a wooden frame. Even the pages in this book come from wood.

For thousands of years, people have made useful and beautiful things from wood. Do-it-yourself carpenters and skilled craftsmen saw, glue, join, and polish wood to make everything from simple toys to concert pianos.

You can create with wood, too. All you need is some wood and a few woodworking tools. You can build a stool to sit on. An old roller skate and a board can take you traveling around your neighborhood. And you can make a musical instrument from ice-cream sticks and wood scraps.

If you've never worked with wood before, now is the time to start. With wood, you can create toys and games and useful objects.

Helpful hints

The following information will help you make the projects in this section. If a special skill is needed, the directions will tell you the page on which that skill is explained. For example: "Saw along these lines (see **sawing,** page 202)." If you do not know how to saw wood, you will find directions on page 202.

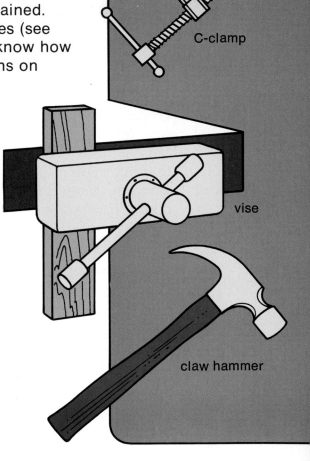

C-clamp

vise

claw hammer

Wood is the basic material used for this section's projects. When you want to work with wood, you should gather the wood before you begin the project.

Your parents or older people you know may have leftover wood scraps you can use. But, always ask their permission before you take the wood.

If someone is building or repairing a house, they will sometimes let you have wood scraps. If you live in an apartment building, the superintendent may be able to help you. You can also get wood scraps free, or for a small charge, at a lumberyard. Ask one of the salesmen if you can look through the scrap barrel.

Sometimes, buying new lumber at a lumberyard is the only way you'll be able to get what you need. Most lumber is cut to a specific width and thickness. Use these measurements to ask for what you want.

For example, a 2 × 4 is a piece of lumber about 2 inches (5 cm) thick and 4 inches (10 cm) wide. Actually, it is a little smaller because the rough wood has been smoothed and evened.

You should also know how long a piece you'll need. Most lumber comes in lengths that are multiples of 2 feet (0.6 m), starting at 4 feet (1.2 m).

Plywood is a special wood that is sold in large sheets. It is made of several layers of thin wood glued together to make a wood "sandwich." If you look at the edge of a piece of plywood, you'll see these layers. The thinnest plywood is $\frac{1}{4}$ inch (7 mm) thick.

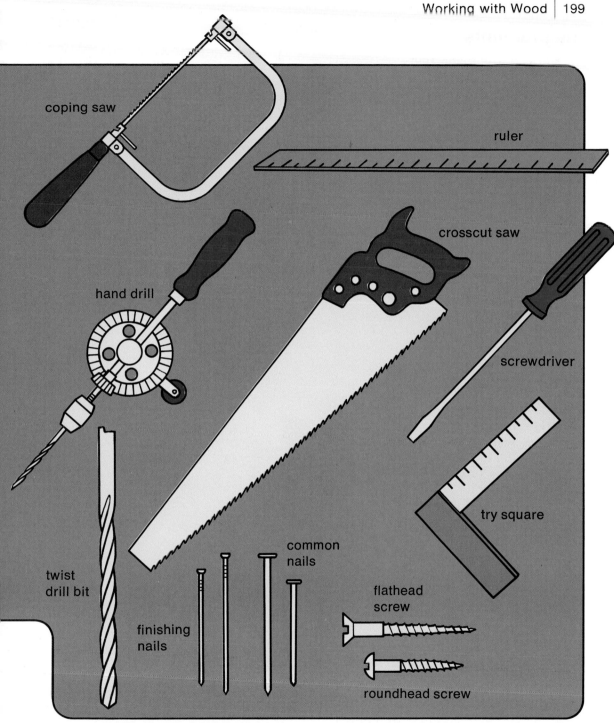

coping saw

ruler

crosscut saw

hand drill

screwdriver

twist drill bit

finishing nails

common nails

flathead screw

try square

roundhead screw

The **woodworking tools** you'll need may have to be borrowed from a grown-up. Always ask permission to use someone else's tools. And be sure to return the tools in good condition and to their proper place.

Warning: Be careful when you use woodworking tools. They are not toys. Follow the directions for using the tools. And don't be afraid to ask a grown-up for help.

(continued on page 200)

Helpful hints

(continued from page 199)

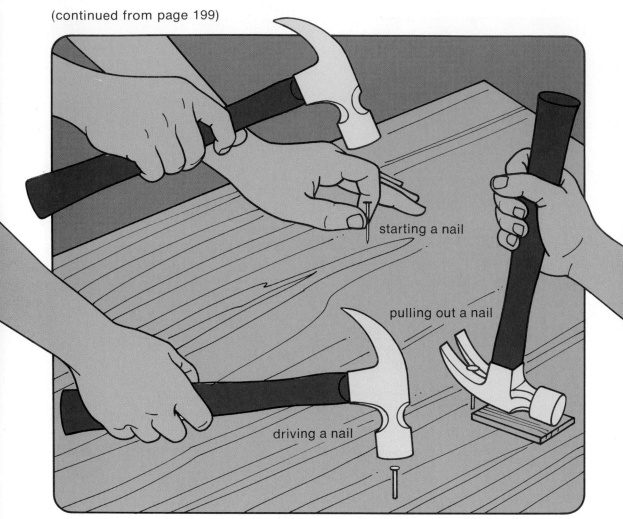

starting a nail

pulling out a nail

driving a nail

Driving nails into wood is the easiest way to fasten pieces of wood together. Make a pencil mark where you want to put the nail. Hold the nail in place with one hand. Hold the hammer near the middle of the handle with your other hand. Tap the nail until it stands up by itself. Then hold the hammer near the end of the handle. Don't hold the nail. Drive the nail all the way into the wood.

If the nail starts to bend, tap it on the side until it is straight. If you can't straighten it, you will have to pull it out and start over.

To pull out the nail, hook the head of the nail in the claw of the hammer. Slide a thin piece of wood under the head of the hammer. Then pull on the handle until the nail comes out.

Remember, use common nails with large flat heads where you don't care if the nail shows. Use finishing nails with tiny heads where you want the nail to be less visible and even with the surface of the wood. The nail should be long enough to go through one piece of wood and part way into the second piece, and thin enough not to split the wood.

Driving screws into pieces of wood to fasten them together makes a stronger joint than one fastened with nails. Always use a screwdriver that fits the slot as tightly as possible, and coat the threads of the screw with soft soap. This will make the job easier.

To drive small screws into soft wood, tap the screw with a hammer until the screw stands in the wood by itself. For larger screws, first drill a pilot hole (see **drilling,** page 201). Put the blade of the screwdriver into the screw's slot. Hold the tip of the screwdriver with one hand. Grip the handle of the screwdriver with your other hand. Turn the screw clockwise.

Remember, use flathead screws where you want the screwhead even with the surface of the wood. Use roundhead screws when you want the screwhead to decorate the project. The size screw you use should be long enough to go through one piece of wood and part way into the second piece, and thin enough not to split the wood.

Drilling holes makes it easier to drive screws (and nails if the wood is likely to split). The twist drill bit you use with the hand drill should be a little smaller in diameter (thickness) than the screw or nail you are going to use.

Make a pencil mark where you want the hole. Clamp the wood in a vise, or use C-clamps to attach it to a table. Place the point of the twist drill bit on the pencil mark. Drill with a steady, even pressure.

If you are drilling a hole for a nail, drill through one piece of wood only. If you are going to use a screw, drill the hole through one piece of wood and part way into the second piece.

(continued on page 202)

screwing

drilling

Helpful hints

(continued from page 201)

Squaring is important when you want to cut several pieces of wood from a single board, or when you want to cut two pieces that will fit together evenly. Use a try square to make sure the end of a board is square and to draw lines across a narrow board.

To check for squareness, fit the corner of the board inside the angle of the try square. If there is any open space between the edge of the board and the try square, the board is not square.

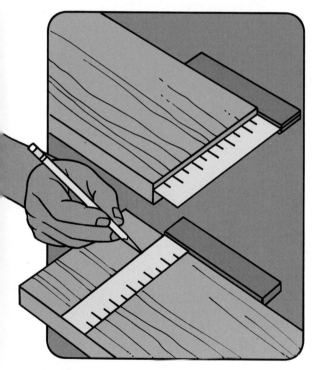

To square the end, use the edge of the try square as a guide and draw a line, as shown. Cut the wood on this line.

Once the board is square, use a ruler to measure the length you need. Use the try square as a guide when drawing the cutting lines. Always check your measurements before you start to saw.

Sawing is easy if you hold the wood firmly. Use a vise or C-clamps to hold small pieces of wood. Rest long pieces on two sawhorses or old chairs, and hold the wood in place with your knee. The piece you are sawing off should stick out beyond the sawhorses.

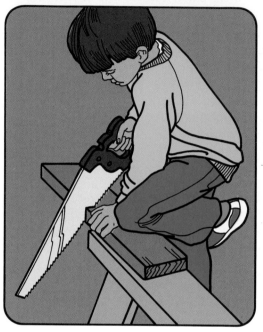

Before you start to saw, mark the cutting line (see **squaring,** page 202). Always work so you can see this line as you saw.

Start the cut with short upstrokes near the handle of the saw. Once the cut is started, you can make long strokes as you push and pull the saw. Put pressure on the downstrokes only. If you cut only on the downstrokes, you will cut faster and not get tired.

You must support the piece of wood you are sawing off, or the board will splinter. If you are cutting off a small piece, reach over the saw and hold the edge of the wood. If the piece is too big for you to support with your hand, put a box under it.

Sanding gives wood a smooth finish. Sandpaper, or flint paper, is marked coarse, medium, and fine. Start sanding with coarse or medium paper and finish with fine paper.

To make sanding easier, wrap the sandpaper around a small block of wood. If the sandpaper is too big for the block, tear it to fit.

Sand with the grain of the wood, not across it. The grain runs in the same direction as the little lines you see in the wood. When you have sanded both sides of the wood, smooth the edges and the corners.

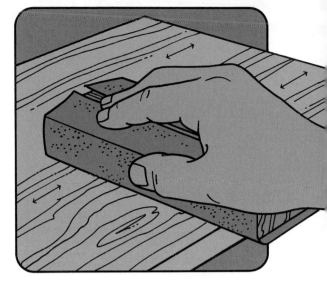

Finishing the wood will change the appearance of the entire project. You can decorate wood with felt-tip pens, paint, or wood stain. Work directly on the bare wood.

To protect your decorations and to give the wood a shiny look, brush on varnish or polyurethane, a plastic varnish. But be very careful. Varnish has two enemies, dust and bubbles.

Dust will leave rough spots on your project. To remove dust, wipe your project with a tack rag before you apply the varnish.

To make a tack rag, pour a little varnish on a piece of old sheet or other cloth that is not fuzzy. Cover your hands with a plastic bag and squeeze the varnish into the rag. Store your tack rag in a closed jar. This will keep the rag from drying out.

Bubbles will also make rough spots on your project. To prevent bubbles, don't shake the can or stir the varnish. If you do, you will make bubbles in the liquid that will brush right onto your project.

When you brush on the varnish, use long even strokes. Brushing too much also causes bubbles. And no matter what you do, once you've got bubbles, they are there to stay.

Clean your brushes in turpentine when you are finished using them. Then wash the bristles with soap and water. Wrap the brushes in paper towels until the bristles are dry.

Captain Billy's tugboat and barge

Materials

- glue (white)
- hammer
- lumber (scrap wood; dowel or old wooden broom handle)
- nails
- paintbrush
- pencil
- ruler
- sandpaper
- saw
- string
- varnish

1 For the hull of the tugboat, use a piece of scrap wood that is longer than it is wide.

2 To make a pointed bow, draw a triangle at one end of the wood, as shown. Do not draw the dashed line.

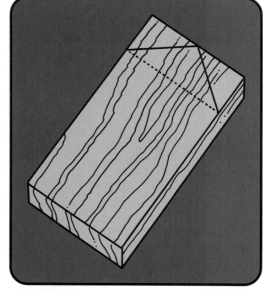

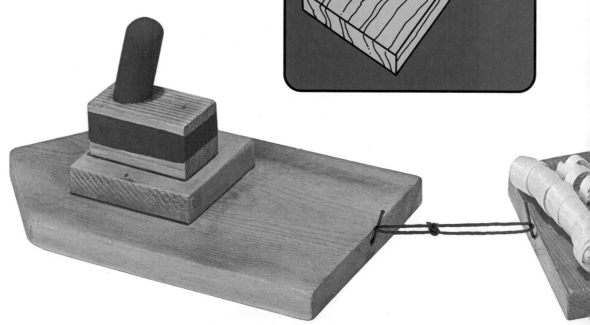

3 Saw along the solid lines (see **sawing,** page 202). Sand the hull (see **sanding,** page 203).

4 To make the pilot house, sand two small scraps of wood and glue them together. Then glue the pilot house to the boat. Put a brick or heavy book on the pilot house. Let the glue dry.

5 For a smokestack, glue a small piece of dowel or old wooden broom handle to the pilot house.

6 For the barge, use a rectangular piece of scrap wood a little larger than the hull of the tugboat. Sand the barge.

7 Put a finish on your tugboat and barge (see **finishing,** page 203).

8 To make hooks so your tugboat can pull the barge, tap a nail into the back of the tugboat and barge. Hammer the nails over, as shown. Use a piece of string to tie the barge to the tugboat.

You can pretend you're Captain Billy as you sail your tugboat and barge in your bathtub or swimming pool.

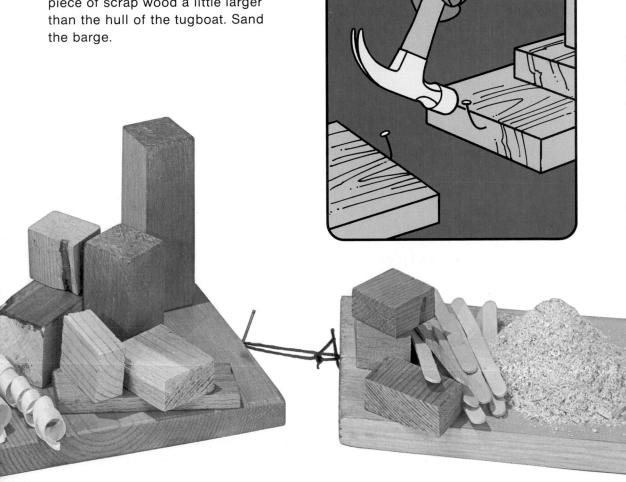

Bamboo wind chimes

Materials

- **bamboo pole**
- **coping saw**
- **hand drill with $\frac{1}{8}$-inch twist drill bit**
- **nail**
- **sandpaper**
- **scissors**
- **string**
- **tape (transparent)**
- **vise**

Bamboo is a giant grass that grows in lands that are very hot and wet. It is stiff, like wood, and has a hollow stem.

1 Saw off six pieces of bamboo (see **sawing,** page 202). Saw above and below the ringed joints so you have six hollow pieces. Sand the ends of each piece (see **sanding,** page 203).

2 Use one piece of bamboo for the crosspiece. Put the crosspiece in a vise, and drill five evenly spaced holes (see **drilling,** page 201).

3 To make the chimes, drill a hole about 1 inch (2.5 cm) from the end of the other bamboo pieces.

4 Hang the chimes from the crosspiece. Cut five pieces of string, each about 8 inches (20 cm) long. Wrap one end of each string with transparent tape. Thread the string through the holes in the crosspiece and chimes, as shown. Tie a knot.

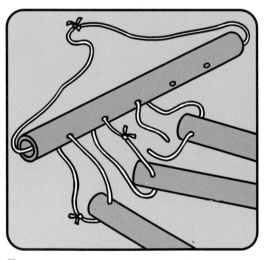

5 Cut off another piece of string about four times as long as the crosspiece. Tie the end of the string to a nail. Then drop the nail and the string through the crosspiece. Take the nail off and tie the ends of the string in a knot.

Picture puzzle

Materials

- **coping saw**
- **glue (white)**
- **paintbrush**
- **pencil**
- **picture (magazine or poster)**
- **plywood** ($\frac{1}{4}$ **inch thick)**
- **sandpaper**
- **varnish**
- **vise**

1 Sand the plywood on both sides and on the edges (see **sanding,** page 203).

2 Glue your picture to the wood. Spread a thin layer of glue on the back of the picture. Then press the picture on the wood. Let the glue dry.

3 Draw the puzzle pieces on the back of the wood. For your first puzzle, make the pieces large and keep the shapes simple.

4 Place the wood in a vise with the puzzle pieces facing you. Slowly and carefully cut out the puzzle pieces (see **sawing,** page 202) with a coping saw. If you use a fine blade (one with more teeth per inch) you will be able to cut very sharp curves.

5 Sand the edges of the pieces.

6 Varnish the puzzle (see **finishing,** page 203). Varnish one side, and let it dry. Then varnish the other side and the edges. Let the varnish dry.

Now try to put your puzzle together.

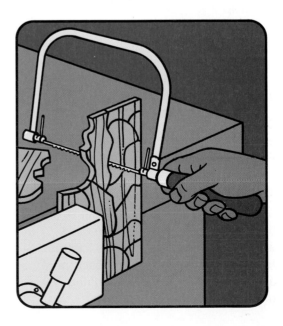

Walking-tall stilts

A long time ago, people used stilts to walk above flooded ground. You can use stilts to make you taller, to help you look over high fences, or to pretend you're the tall man in the circus.

1 To make the poles, saw the 1 × 2 into two lengths. Each piece should stand about 2 inches (5 cm) above your shoulders (see **sawing,** page 202).

2 For the footrests, use two pieces of scrap 2 × 4. The length of the footrest will be the distance you'll stand from the ground. If you've never used stilts before, it's a good idea to make the footrests no more than 12 inches (30 cm) long.

3 Sand the poles and the footrests (see **sanding,** page 203).

4 To nail on the footrests, prop the poles with a 2 × 4 scrap. Make sure the bottom of the pole is flush, or even, with the bottom of the footrest. Hammer five nails through each pole and into the footrest (see **driving nails,** page 200).

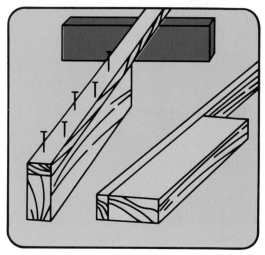

5 Lean against a wall or ask a friend to hold the stilts until you get your balance. Grip the poles so that they are **behind** your shoulders. To walk, pull the stilts up against your feet as you shift your weight from one leg to the other.

African thumb piano

Materials

- **crosscut saw**
- **glue (white)**
- **hand drill with twist drill bit**
- **ice-cream sticks (four)**
- **lumber ($\frac{1}{4}$ inch plywood, scrap blocks, and thin strips)**
- **pencil**
- **ruler**
- **sandpaper**
- **screwdriver**
- **screws, roundhead (two)**

1 For the top and bottom of the piano, cut out two rectangles from the plywood (see **sawing,** page 202). Each piece should be about 6 inches (15 cm) wide and 8 inches (20 cm) long. Sand the sides and edges of both pieces (see **sanding,** page 203).

2 Cut four blocks. Each block should be about 1 inch (2.5 cm) thick and 1 inch (2.5 cm) long on each side.

Sand the blocks. Then glue them between the top and bottom pieces. Put a brick or heavy book on the top piece. Let the glue dry.

3 Cut three crossbars (A, B, and C), each about $\frac{1}{2}$ inch (12 mm) wide and 6 inches (15 cm) long. One crossbar should be a little thicker than the others. Sand the crossbars.

Glue crossbars A and B to the top of the piano, about $\frac{3}{4}$ inch (2 cm) apart. Use the thick crossbar for crossbar A.

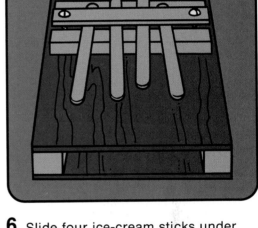

4 Drill a hole about $\frac{1}{2}$ inch (12 mm) from each end of crossbar C (see **drilling,** page 201).

5 Screw crossbar C to the piano top between crossbars A and B (see **driving screws,** page 201). Use roundhead screws that will not go all the way through the piano top. Do not tighten the screws yet.

6 Slide four ice-cream sticks under crossbar C. Position the sticks on crossbars A and B so the ends resting on crossbar A are different lengths. This will make each one sound different. Tighten the screws to hold the sticks in place.

To play your African thumb piano, hold the piano in both hands. Snap the ice-cream sticks with your thumbs until you create a rhythm you like.

Most African music is played on drums, but stringed instruments and woodwinds are also used to make pleasing sounds and rhythms.

Old-time skate scooter

Materials

- **common nails
  (4d and 8d or larger)**
- **crosscut saw**
- **flat, 4-inch L brackets
  and screws**
- **hammer**
- **hand drill
  with twist drill bit**
- **lumber
  (6-foot 2 × 4 or two 3-foot
  2 × 4's; 1 × 1; and scrap
  wood)**
- **pencil**
- **ruler**
- **old roller skate (adjustable)**
- **screwdriver**
- **screws (two)**
- **vise**

1 Measure the distance from the floor to your waist. Saw two pieces of 2 × 4 to this length (see **sawing**, page 202). Sand the wood (see **sanding**, page 203).

2 Use one old roller skate for the scooter's wheels. Remove the ankle strap and the toe holders. Then unscrew the middle screw and take the skate apart.

3 Nail the skate wheels near the ends of one of the 2 × 4 pieces. Place the nails through the holes in the skate or next to the skate. Hammer 8d or larger common nails halfway into the 2 × 4 (see **driving nails,** page 200). Then hammer the nails over, as shown.

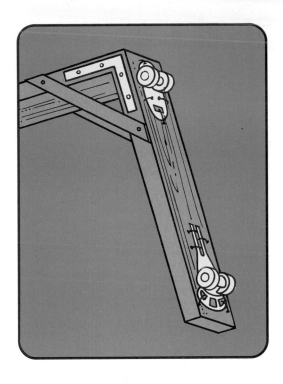

4 Put the parts of the scooter together, as shown. Screw flat L brackets on each side of the scooter (see **driving screws,** page 201).

Use two pieces of scrap lumber about 10 inches (25 cm) long, 2 inches (5 cm) wide, and $\frac{1}{4}$ inch (7 mm) thick for braces. Cut the ends of the braces on a slant. Sand the braces. Then nail them to the scooter, as shown.

5 Use a 14-inch (35-cm) length of 1 × 1 for the handle. Make a mark 6 inches from each end. Put the handle in a vise and drill holes through it at the marks (see **drilling,** page 201). Sand the handle smooth.

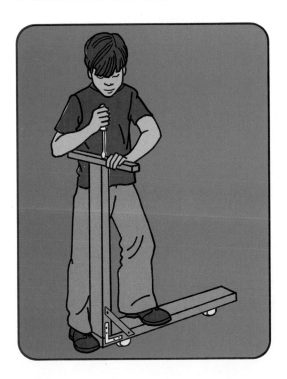

6 Screw the handle to the scooter. Drive the screws through the handle until you can see the tips of the screws on the other side. Hold the scooter steady with your foot, as shown. Place the handle on the scooter and tighten the screws.

7 Put a finish on your scooter (see **finishing,** page 203). Be careful not to paint or varnish the wheels.

Stool

1 Square one end of the 1×10 and the 1×4 pine boards (see **squaring,** page 202).

2 Cut the pieces for the stool. Measure and saw one piece at a time (see **sawing,** page 202).

Use the 1×10 for the top and legs. For the top, cut off a piece 14 inches (35 cm) long. Cut off two pieces, each 8 inches (20 cm) long, for the legs.

Use the 1×4 for the crosspieces. Cut off two crosspieces, each 14 inches (35 cm) long.

3 Sand all the pieces (see **sanding,** page 203).

Materials

- **crosscut saw**
- **finishing nails (4d)**
- **glue (white)**
- **hammer**
- **lumber (1 × 10 and 1 × 4 pine boards)**
- **paintbrush**
- **pencil**
- **ruler**
- **sandpaper**
- **try square**
- **varnish**

4 Attach the legs to the top of the stool, as shown. Use both glue and 4d finishing nails. Place the nails about 2 inches (5 cm) apart. Wipe off any glue that squeezes out of the joints. Let the glue dry.

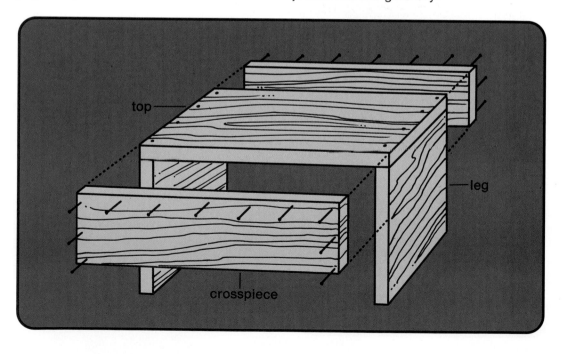

top

leg

crosspiece

5 Attach the crosspieces to the legs and top of the stool, as shown. Use both glue and 4d finishing nails. Place the nails about 2 inches (5 cm) apart. Wipe off any glue that squeezes out of the joints. Let the glue dry.

6 Put a finish on your stool (see **finishing,** page 203).

You can use your stool when you watch television or when you want to reach high places. If you use wider crosspieces, you can make a box.

On your own

Here are more things you can make with wood.

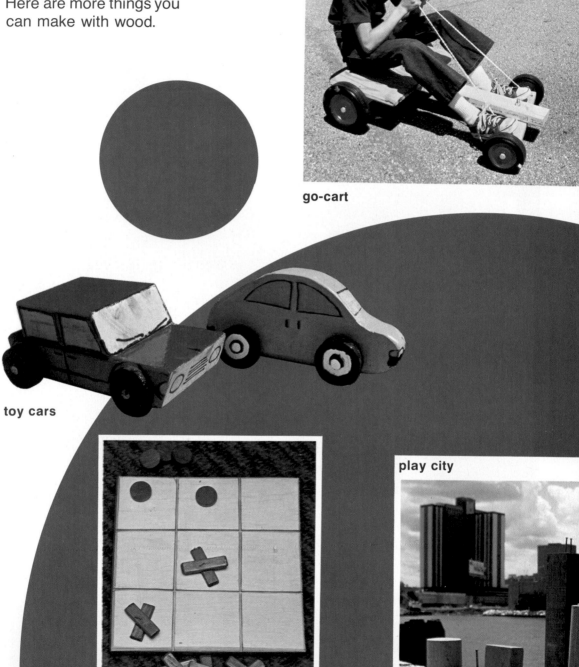

go-cart

toy cars

play city

tick-tack-toe

hanging tool box

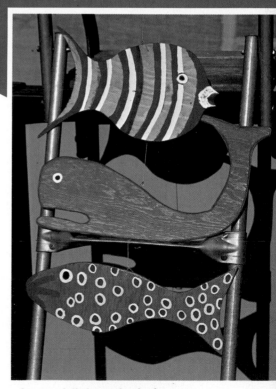

plywood fish and whale

Gifts to Give

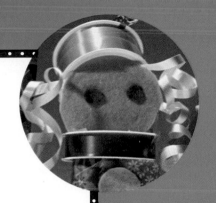

Gifts are fun to give! And special hand-made gifts are even more fun than the gifts you can buy in a store. Made-to-order gifts say "You're special. And I made a special gift just for you."

When you think about making and giving gifts, think first about the person to whom you are going to give them. Try to remember what he or she likes. What are his interests? What are her favorite colors? What might he need? What have you heard her talking about lately? When you've answered these questions, you're ready to plan a gift-making project.

Look through the gift ideas in this section. You'll find gifts for grown-ups and gifts for children. Then look through the rest of the book. Many of the projects and ideas in the other sections can be given as gifts, too.

And when you've finished making a gift, wrap it up in a perky package, make a card to say "hello," and pop on a bouncy bow. Your gift is ready to give!

Easy gift ideas

Treasure pets will delight young and old alike. They'll hold candy, jewelry, a ball of string or yarn, or any small trinkets that will fit inside.

Start with a plastic pantyhose egg. Open the egg and cover each half with papier-mâché pulp (see **papier-mâché pulp,** page 89). But, don't cover the edge where the halves connect. Mold the body, head, and legs with the pulp. Use toothpicks to strengthen the legs and neck, if needed. Let dry.

To decorate the pet, paint each half with tempera paint. When the paint is dry, varnish each half. Let dry completely. Finally, glue on felt eyes and any other decorations you wish.

Fruit-juice-can banks are perfect presents for the people on your gift list who like to save for a rainy day. Use enamel paint to decorate a rinsed-out fruit-juice can—the kind with a pull-off foil seal. Glue on buttons, feathers, beans, rice, yarn, or pieces of paper to make designs. The can opening becomes the money slot. When the bank is full, it can be opened with a can opener.

Cloth-covered boxes can be used by many people for many things. They can be used as trinket boxes, sewing boxes, desk caddies, or yarn or string dispensers. Simply glue cloth, such as felt or burlap, onto a cardboard box.

First, cut out any slits or holes you might want (see **inside cuts,** page 37). Then, cover the sides of the box with cloth. Leave a little extra cloth to fold over the edges. Then cover the bottom. Use a different kind of cloth to cover the top and its sides. When the glue is dry, cut out any material covering the slits or holes. Finally, glue on decorations or add a few fancy stitches (see **Helpful hints,** page 154).

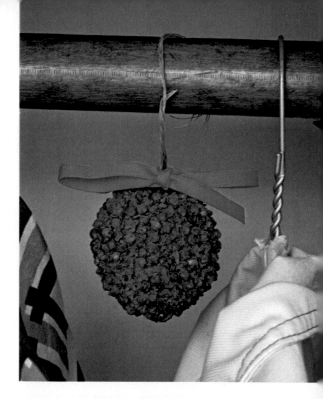

Spicy pomanders will make the clothes in a drawer or closet smell fresh. You can make this pomander with an orange and spices you find in your kitchen.

Push whole cloves into an orange. Sprinkle cinnamon on the orange and wrap it in wax paper. Wait one week. Then take off the wax paper. Fold some picture-frame wire in half, and push it through the orange. Bend back the two ends and push them into the orange.

Noteboards are popular gifts that can be used anywhere in the house.

Glue two pieces of corrugated cardboard together, with the corrugation running in opposite directions. Cover the cardboard with felt. Then glue felt decorations near the border and attach a picture hook to the back.

Candy cuties will delight everyone's sweet tooth! They're made with Styrofoam and wrapped candy.

Start with a 4-inch (10-cm) or larger Styrofoam ball for the body. Cut off the bottom of the ball so it won't roll. Use stick pins to attach wrapped candies to the body. Use a 1-inch (2.5-cm), or larger, Styrofoam ball or egg to make the head. Attach the head with a small piece of pipe cleaner. Pin on felt hands, feet, wings, and feathers. Then add any other felt and pipe-cleaner decorations you like.

Bottles and pots will liven up any window sill. Decorated bottles can be used as vases, oil and vinegar jars, bubble-bath and shaving-lotion bottles, and as candleholders. And, of course, a decorated flower pot would make any plant smile just a little bit more.

Paint bottles with enamel paint and flower pots with either enamel or tempera paint. If you are painting a flower pot, you may want to paint the inside, too. When the paint is dry, brush on one or two coats of varnish.

Trays are gifts grown-ups like. This one is made from an old picture frame.

Take the glass out of an old picture frame and set it aside. Sand the frame. Nail a wooden package handle (the kind stores use to help you carry bulky packages) to each end of the frame. Paint the frame and the handles. Then varnish. When the varnish is dry, put the glass back in the frame. Place a picture, a pretty piece of cloth, a stitchery picture (see page 158), or a woven tapestry (see page 192) in the frame. Slip a piece of heavy cardboard into the frame to hold the picture and glass in place. Finally, glue felt to the bottom of the tray.

Fun clothes hangers will brighten up anyone's closet. Sand a wooden hanger (see **sanding,** page 203). Then decorate the hanger with paint or decoupage (see page 230). Give the hanger a coat of varnish (see **finishing,** page 203).

See-through pictures are happy holiday gifts. All you need is gel medium, which you can buy in an art store or craft shop.

Brush twelve coats of gel on a magazine picture or on a crayon picture you have drawn on shiny shelf paper. Let the gel dry between coats. When the gel dries after the last coat, soak the picture in water until you can peel off the paper. Then, presto! You will see that, like magic, the picture is stuck in the gel.

Gifts for sports fans

Tennis racket covers are good gifts for both grown-ups and kids who play tennis. Trace the tennis racket and part of the handle on a piece of paper. Add $\frac{1}{2}$ inch (17 mm) all around. Cut out two pieces of felt, using the pattern as a guide. Cut a felt strip $1\frac{3}{4}$ inches (43 mm) wide and long enough to go around the racket.

Use yarn to sew the bottom piece of the cover to the strip (see **overcast stitch,** page 156). Then sew the top to the strip. Along one top edge, leave an opening large enough to slip the racket inside the cover. Overcast the open edge for decoration.

For ties, make eight 7-inch (15-cm) braids (see **braid,** page 181). Sew four braids on the side and top of the cover, along the open edge. Glue on felt decorations.

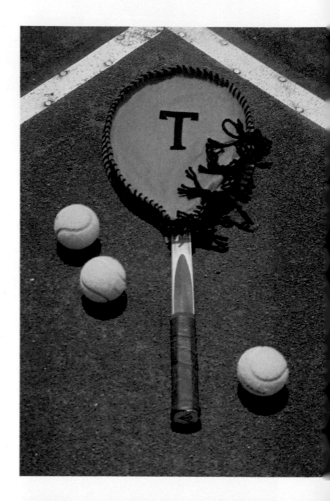

Sports towels can be used by anybody who plays a sport. Decorate the towel with a bowling ball and pins for a bowler, clubs and flags for a golfer, bats and balls for a baseball player, rackets and balls for a tennis buff, or a fish for someone who likes to go fishing.

Cut out the decorations from soft cotton cloth. Pin them to a hand towel, turning under the edges. Sew the shapes to the towel (see **overcast stitch,** page 156).

Golf club mitts to cover the heads of the wood clubs are the perfect gift for a golfer. You can make these mitts from 12-inch (30-cm) felt squares. You'll need two squares for each mitt.

First, find out which woods your golfer has—No. 1, 2, 3, 4, or 5.

Cut out seven felt "I's" and two "V's" to make the numerals I, II, III, IV, V. Glue a numeral to the front half of each mitt. Then make four 7-inch (17-cm) braids (see **braid,** page 181). Fold each braid in half. To make loops, sew one folded braid to the back half of each mitt, about 1 inch (2.5 cm) from the top.

Place the two halves of each mitt with the wrong sides together. Overcast the mitts with yarn along the sides and top (see **overcast stitch,** page 156).

To tie the mitts together, make one 24-inch (60-cm) braid. Thread the braid through the loops on the mitts and tie the ends together.

Baubles, bangles, and beads

Fruit pins look good enough to eat. Cut out fruit shapes from doubled pieces of felt. Use embroidery thread to sew the pieces together (see **backstitch,** page 156). Leave a small opening. Stuff the shape with cotton. Then close the opening. Stitch a safety pin to the back. If you want to add leaves, make them separately and then sew them to the fruit shapes.

Animal crackers parade right out of the box and onto a shirt or hat brim. Varnish both sides of an animal cracker. Let dry. Varnish the cracker two more times. When the varnish is dry, glue a small safety pin to the back of the cracker. If you want, paint the cracker after you varnish it. Then varnish it again. Please, these animal crackers are not for eating.

Papier-mâché jewelry will delight young and old alike.

Make beads in all kinds of shapes out of papier-mâché pulp (see **papier-mâché pulp,** page 89). Use a toothpick to poke holes in the beads. When the papier-mâché is dry, paint the beads and varnish them. String necklaces on heavy thread and bracelets on elastic thread.

The bangle bracelets are made with papier-mâché strips (see **strip papier-mâché,** page 88). Bend and tape a piece of thin cardboard into a circle large enough to slip over the person's hand. Cover the circle with papier-mâché strips. When the bracelet is dry, paint and varnish it. Or, decorate it with decoupage (see page 230).

Make a brooch with papier-mâché pulp. Press the pulp into the shape you want. When it is dry, decorate the brooch with paint or decoupage, and then varnish it. Glue a small safety pin to the back.

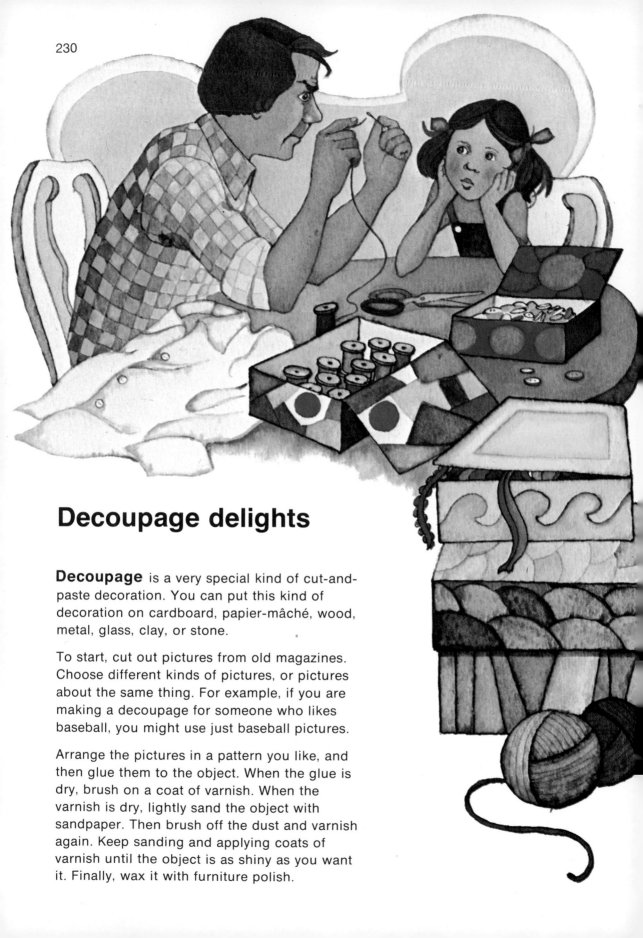

Decoupage delights

Decoupage is a very special kind of cut-and-paste decoration. You can put this kind of decoration on cardboard, papier-mâché, wood, metal, glass, clay, or stone.

To start, cut out pictures from old magazines. Choose different kinds of pictures, or pictures about the same thing. For example, if you are making a decoupage for someone who likes baseball, you might use just baseball pictures.

Arrange the pictures in a pattern you like, and then glue them to the object. When the glue is dry, brush on a coat of varnish. When the varnish is dry, lightly sand the object with sandpaper. Then brush off the dust and varnish again. Keep sanding and applying coats of varnish until the object is as shiny as you want it. Finally, wax it with furniture polish.

Decoupage boxes can be used to hold stationery, jewelry, cards, or trinkets. These handsome boxes are made from cigar boxes lined with felt.

Open the box and glue pictures on all six sides. If you're using a wooden box with hinges, don't cover the hinges. When the glue is dry, open the box and varnish it. Then glue felt to the inside of the box. If you want, you can glue a felt loop to the top.

Decoupage key rings are popular gifts for moms and dads as well as for boys and girls.

Use a coping saw to cut out any shape you choose from $\frac{1}{4}$-inch plywood (see **sawing,** page 202). Drill a small hole about $\frac{1}{2}$ inch (18 mm) from the edge of the shape (see **drilling,** page 201). Sand the edges and both sides of the shape (see **sanding,** page 203). If you want, stain the shape with wood stain. Glue a small picture to the shape and varnish it. Slip a key chain through the hole. Or, make a necklace by putting a leather shoelace through the hole.

Ideas with colors, cloth, and thread

Potato printing on cloth is a creative way to make unusual presents everyone will like. You can print T-shirts, scarves, tablecloths, napkins, place mats, and wallhangings. Or, you can print cloth to make into pillows or stuffed toys.

Potato printing on cloth is done just like potato printing on paper (see **potato prints,** page 80). But, you must use special textile paints that won't wash out. You can buy these paints in art, hobby, and craft shops. Be very careful when you print with this paint. Follow the instructions on the package. Stains and mistakes will not wash out.

When you're finished printing and the paint is dry, use a warm iron to press the fabric. Press each side for about five minutes.

If you're printing a shirt, put several layers of newspaper inside the shirt before you start to print.

Tie-dyeing is a special way of dyeing cloth to get patterns and designs. Tie-dyed presents, such as T-shirts, scarves, tablecloths and napkins, place mats, and wallhangings make creative, one-of-a-kind gifts.

Gather the cloth in several places. Then wind rubber bands or tie string around the bunched-up cloth. You can tie the bunched cloth once, twice, or as many times as you choose. Each time you tie the cloth an extra time or a different way, you'll get a different design.

Dye the cloth in no-boil fabric dye. Make the dye solution stronger than the instructions tell you by mixing more dye with less water.

Put the cloth into the dye. Let the cloth soak until it is a little darker than the color you want. Then wring it out. To make tie-dye projects with several different colors, dip the bunched and tied ends of the dyed cloth in different color dyes up to the first, second, or third knots. Wring out each bunch after you have dyed it.

Finally, rinse the cloth in cold water until the water is clear. Untie the cloth and hang it up to dry. Then press it with a warm iron.

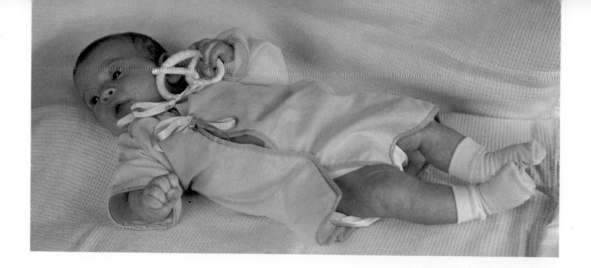

Kimono tops will please the mother of any baby up to the age of two. You'll need $\frac{7}{8}$ yard (80 cm) of cotton or flannel, 1 yard (90 cm) of ribbon, and double-fold seam binding.

Cut the cloth so it is about 30 inches (80 cm) long and 24 inches (60 cm) wide. Fold the cloth in half the short way. Draw and cut out the kimono and the neck opening so it looks like the one in the picture. Then cut a slit down the front of the kimono.

With the right sides of the cloth together, sew the side seams and the sleeve seams (see **backstitch,** page 156). Make the seams about $\frac{5}{8}$ inch (2 cm) wide. Where the side seams turn into the sleeve seams, make little cuts in the seam from the edge of the cloth up to the thread.

Pin double-fold seam binding around the neck opening. Sew it with the backstitch. If you have difficulty doing this, ask a grown-up for help.

Hem the front slit, sleeves, and the bottom of the kimono. Turn under a $\frac{1}{2}$-inch (1.7-cm) hem and pin it down. Tuck under the raw edges to make a little roll. Sew the roll down (see **hemming stitch,** page 156). Or, sew double-fold seam binding around the edges like you did around the neck.

Sew ribbons on each side of the front slit. Add any decorations you like.

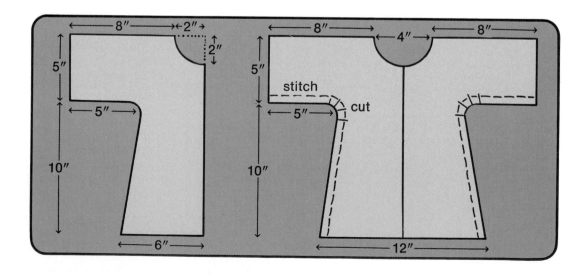

Stuffed animals will keep babies, teen-agers, and everyone in-between company when the party is over. Calico Cat, Checked Puppy, and Waddly Duck will bring a smile to even the most hard-to-please person. You can stitch them up in no time.

Cut out the shape from a piece of doubled cloth. With the right sides of the cloth together, sew around the shape (see **backstitch,** page 156). Leave an opening so you can push in the stuffing. Wherever the seams curve, make little cuts in the seam from the edge of the cloth to the thread. Be careful not to cut the thread. Push the shape through the opening so the right sides are out.

Stuff the shape with shredded foam. Then turn in the edges along the opening and sew it closed with the backstitch.

Sew or glue on eyes, a nose, and a mouth, and any other decorations you like.

Gifts of games

Games are fun-time gifts for everyone.
Although some games are strictly for
children and others are better for adults,
both adults and children will enjoy playing
these games. When you give a game as a
gift, remember to include the rules.

Puzzle blocks will keep people of
all ages amused for hours. These
blocks are made from wooden blocks
covered with magazine and greeting-
card pictures. You will need six pictures
—one for each side of the blocks.
Buy a set of wooden building blocks.
Fill in all the low parts around the
raised letters with white glue. Let
the glue dry.

Arrange the blocks in a square or
rectangle. Tie a string around the
blocks to hold them in place. Glue a
picture to the top of the blocks. When
the glue is dry, ask a grown-up to help
you cut the blocks apart with a sharp
knife. To trim off the picture's rough
edges, cut around each block with a
scissors. Glue a picture on each side
of the blocks.

Nine Men's Morris has been played for about four hundred years! This game can be as difficult to play as an adult wishes to make it, yet it is simple enough for children to play. Playing instructions are on page 293.

You can make a board for playing Nine Men's Morris from a piece of $\frac{3}{4}$-inch plywood or from a piece of scrap wood that is 1 inch (2.5 cm) thick. Read the **Helpful hints** on pages 198-203 before you start.

Cut the wood so it is about 9 or 10 inches (25 cm) square. Then sand the wood. Drill twenty-four holes in the board. Paint lines connecting the holes. Use eighteen golf tees for the playing pieces. Saw off the pointed tips. Sand the tees. Then paint nine pieces one color, and the other nine pieces a different color. Varnish.

Felt game boards are easy to make, interesting to touch, and can be rolled up and taken on a trip.

To make a game board, use one of your games as a pattern. Use a large piece of felt for the background. Cut out the board's design from small pieces of felt. Lay all the pieces on the background to make sure they'll fit. Then glue them to the background. Glue small pieces to larger ones first.

Use painted golf tees for playing pieces (see **Nine Men's Morris**, above). Buy a pair of dice in a variety store. If you choose a game with cards, paint or print them (see **potato prints**, page 80).

Paint a canister to hold the board and playing pieces (see page 238).

Kitchen capers

Canister sets can be used to hold flour, sugar, coffee, tea, nails, screws, crayons, buttons, or anything else you want to collect and keep in one place.

These canisters are made from coffee cans with plastic lids. Wash the cans and lids and remove any paper labels. Give the cans three coats of enamel paint. Then paint a design and labels on the cans.

Kitchen hangers hold potholders and mitts. Decorate a wooden spoon with tempera paint and fabric scraps. Varnish the wood that shows. Drill holes for the hanging cord (see **drilling,** page 201). Then screw threaded hooks into the handle. Tap each hook into the handle with a hammer. Turn and tighten the hooks. Thread the hanging cord or string through the holes and tie a knot.

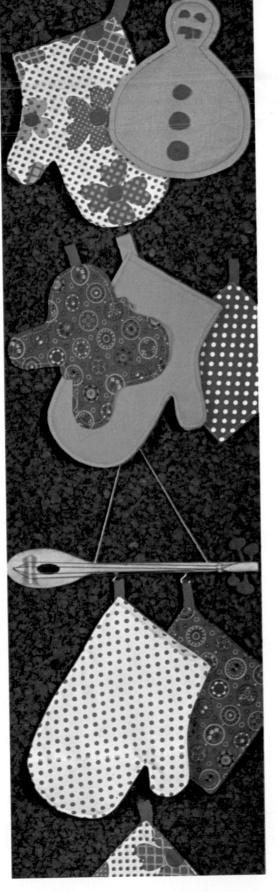

Potholders and mitts will make any cook happy.

To make the potholders, cut out the potholder shape from a doubled piece of felt or quilted cotton. Cut out the same shape from a piece of flannel or terry cloth toweling. Cut this shape a little smaller.

To make a loop, sew a folded piece of fabric, cord, or seam binding to the wrong side of one of the felt or cotton pieces (see **backstitch,** page 156). Then make a "sandwich" with the three pieces of material. Put the terry cloth or flannel in the middle. Pin the pieces together. If you are using material that ravels, turn in the edges first. Use the backstitch or the overcast stitch to sew around the potholder (see **backstitch** and **overcast stitch,** page 156). Sew on any decorations or fancy stitches you like.

To make the mitt, make two large mitten-shaped potholders. Then sew the two potholders together.

Whimsical wrap-ups

When you've taken the time to make a special gift for a special person, you'll want to wrap the gift in an extra-special way. It's just as much fun to wrap the gift as it is to make it. You can key the gift-wrapping to the person's interest, or you can let the wrapping give a hint about the gift.

You can make unusual gift-wrappings with the odds-and-ends left over from your craft projects. Wrap presents in

plain tissue paper, fancy wrapping paper, the classified ads, or the funny pages. Try magazine pictures, construction paper, wallpaper, and grocery bags. Decorate the wrapping paper with paper clips, felt, string, lace, yarn, paint, potato prints, or dried leaves and flowers.

If you wrap the box and lid separately, the box can be used to hold trinkets or reused at another time for a gift.

Wrapping Without a Box

or

Wrapping a Box

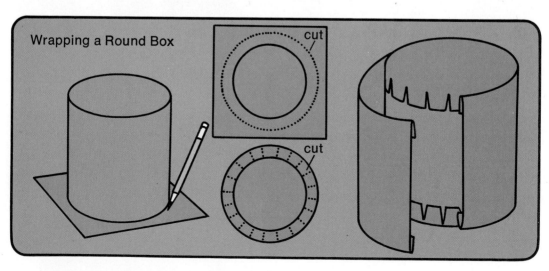

Wrapping a Round Box

cut

cut

Cards that say "You're special"

Greeting cards should be as special as the people who are going to receive them. That's why the best cards are cards you make yourself. No one can say what you want to say, and no one can draw what you want to draw, better than you.

Construction paper is the best paper to use for a greeting card. Decorating the front of the card is a little project in itself. You will find many ideas in the Fun with Paper, Paint and Print, and Nature Crafts sections.

Inside the card, write a special message for the person and add more decorations.

When you receive a gift, you can make a special card to say "thank you." Decorate the front of the card so it looks like the present you received. Write a note to thank the person who gave you the gift. Tell him or her how you are going to use the present.

Dear Terry,
Thank you for the stuffed doggie. I named him Ruff and took him to bed with me that same night! Next to you, Ruff's going to be my best friend.
Love,
Lee

Let's Dress Up

Guess who? Guess who? Is that an owl from the zoo? No! Look again! It's really Ben!

Who is this witch, so fierce and scary? Good grief! It's Patricia-Mary!

It's fun to dress up in a costume—to pretend you're someone else. You can dress up on rainy days and holidays. Or you might go to a party or act in a play where you'll need to wear a costume.

Do you want to be Robin Hood, Maid Marian, or Friar Tuck? Or would you rather dress up like an angel or a beautiful butterfly? On the next pages, you'll find all these, plus many other dress-up ideas. And don't forget to look through your other *Childcraft* volumes for more costume ideas.

What kind of costume will you wear? Do you think your costume will fool anyone into thinking you're not you? Let's find out. Let's dress up!

Pretty Lady

Gypsy
Fortuneteller

Spy

Costume Box: Look at all the people you can be! All you have to do is ask your mom and dad if they have any old clothes, jewelry, and makeup you can have. Keep these things in a special costume box and you'll be all ready to play "dress up" on a rainy day. **Pretty Lady:** Dress up in your mother's old clothes and makeup. **Spy:** Wear a trench coat and your father's old hat. Carry a small box painted to look like a two-way radio. **Gypsy Fortuneteller:** Wear a fancy blouse, lots of petticoats, a skirt, a blanket, and a kerchief. Add jewelry. Carry a deck of cards to tell fortunes. **Johnny Appleseed:** Dress in raggedy old clothes and an old hat. Carry a shoulder purse to hold the appleseeds. **Hobo:** Wear raggedy old clothes and

Pirate

Hobo

Clown

Johnny Appleseed

carry your things in a kerchief tied to a stick. For makeup, ask a grown-up to help you burn the end of a cork. Rub the burnt cork on your face.
Pirate: Dress in raggedy old clothes. Wear an earring, paper moustache, and an eyepatch. Tie a kerchief on your head and carry a cardboard sword. Wear burnt cork makeup (see Hobo). **Clown:** Wear your father's old

pajamas, work gloves, and a worn-out pair of shoes. To make a wig, cut off the foot of an old sock. Tie one end of the tube with string and turn it inside out. Sew yarn all over the tube. Cover your face with cold cream and pat on flour. Outline and color your mouth, eyes, nose, and cheeks with lipstick. With an eyebrow pencil, draw heavy eyebrows and dark lines under your eyes.

Ghoulish Ghost

Scary Skeleton

Wicked Witch

Scary Skeleton: Wear a leotard, tights, and gloves. Stick on strips of white reflector tape as bones. For the hat, cut off the foot of an old sock. Tie one end of the tube with string and turn it inside out. For makeup, use burnt cork (see Hobo, page 246), cover the rest of your face with cold cream and pat on flour. **Ghoulish Ghost:** Wear a leotard, tights, gloves, and sheet. See Scary Skeleton

for makeup. **Wicked Witch:** Make a basic costume with long, wide sleeves (see page 256). Cut off the feet of old nylon stockings. Starting at the bottom of the costume, sew on the stockings. Wear a brimmed hat with a cone crown (see page 258). Draw wrinkle lines with an eyebrow pencil. **Angel:** Make a long basic costume with wide sleeves (see page 256). Sew on tinsel garland

Devil

Shepherd

Angel

with the overcast stitch (see page 156). Make cardboard wings and cover them with foil. Tie them on with string and garland. For the halo, use 4 feet (1.2 cm) of wire covered with foil.
Devil: Wear red tights. Make a tunic with long sleeves (see page 256). For the hood, make a sack costume with pointed horns (see page 257). Cut out a face hole. Stuff the horns with

cotton. For the tail, make a yarn braid (see page 178). Push wire through it. Rub burnt cork on your face (see Hobo, page 246). Carry a cardboard pitchfork.
Shepherd: Make a long basic costume with wide sleeves (see page 256). For the hat, use a piece of cloth and a felt headband. Carry a blanket over your shoulder and a cardboard shepherd's crook in your hand.

Owl

Butterfly

Beagle

Penguin

Lamb

Ladybug

Beagle: Make a sack costume (see page 257). Sew on felt ears with the backstitch (see page 156). Paint the spots and face with tempera paint. For the tail, make a yarn braid (see page 181). **Owl:** Make a sack costume (see page 257). Make felt feathers, each about 6 inches (15 cm) long and 4 inches (10 cm) wide. Paint the lines with tempera paint. Starting at the hem, sew on rows of feathers with the running stitch (see page 155). Do not sew feathers around the eyeholes. Sew on a felt beak and eyes with the overcast stitch (see page 156). Cut out eyeholes. **Penguin:** Make a black felt sack costume (see page 257). Glue on or paint the wings, feet, and breast. Sew on a felt beak and eyes with the overcast stitch (see page 156). Cut out eyeholes. **Lamb:** Make a white terry cloth sack costume (see page 257). Draw a nose and mouth, or glue on ones made of felt. Sew on felt ears and a tail of braided yarn (see Beagle). **Butterfly:** Wear a leotard and tights. Make a pair of cardboard wings. Color or paint both sides. Glue and tape cloth shoulder straps and a waistband to the front of the wings. For the antennae, cut holes in a felt headband, two holes for each antenna. Push pipe cleaners through the holes and glue in place. **Ladybug:** Wear a leotard and tights. Cut out two pieces of red felt in the shape of rounded squares. Sew the two pieces together using the backstitch (see page 156), but leave an opening. Stuff with rags or crumpled newspaper and stitch the opening. Glue on felt spots and a stripe. From black cloth, cut out two shoulder straps and a waistband. Use the backstitch to sew these on. Wear antennae (see Butterfly).

Robin Hood: Wear a leotard and tights. Make a felt tunic with short sleeves and a separate collar (see page 256). Wear a soft cap with a feather (see page 258). **Maid Marian:** Make a long basic costume with wide, pointed sleeves and a front neck slit (see page 256). Tie a sash around your waist. Wear a cone crown with a scarf tucked into the end (see page 259). **Friar Tuck:** Make a long basic costume with wide sleeves (see page 256). Wear a rope belt. For the collar, make a sack costume that is just big enough for your head (see page 257). Cut out a face hole and pull it over your head. **Pilgrim Boy:** Wear jeans and white knee socks. Make a tunic with long sleeves and a front opening (see page 256). Sew snaps along the opening. Paint or sew on buttons. Make a square collar and cuffs of felt (see page 257). For the hat, make a brimmed hat with a cone crown (see page 258). Measure up 9 inches (23 cm) from the brim and draw a line. Cut on this line (see inside cuts, page 37). Finish like a flat crown (see page 259). **Pilgrim Girl:** Make a long basic costume with long, narrow sleeves (see page 256). Add a square collar and cuffs of felt (see page 257). For the apron, use a piece of cloth 24 inches (60 cm) wide and long enough to reach your knees. Hem it on three sides. Gather it on the fourth side with the running stitch (see page 155). Use the backstitch to sew the gathered edge to a sash (see page 156). Wear a soft cap with the seam running from ear to ear.

Maid Marian

Robin Hood

Friar Tuck

Pilgrim Boy

Pilgrim Girl

Robot

Rocket

Clock

Astronaut

Clock: Wear a leotard, tights, and a sandwich board. To make the sandwich board, cut out two large cardboard circles. Decorate the circles to look like the face and back of a clock. Glue and tape felt shoulder straps to the circles. Glue two strips of cardboard between the circles, to cover each side of your body. Wear a stiff cap (see page 258). **Robot:** Wear dark jeans and a shirt, boots, and rubber gloves. Cut out holes in a cardboard carton for your head and arms (see inside cuts, page 37). Cut an eye slit in a smaller carton for your head. Glue on different things to look like knobs and dials. **Astronaut:** Wear long-sleeved pajamas, rubber gloves, and boots. Add strips of silver-gray reflector tape. Glue on felt patches. For the helmet, cut a strip of cardboard about 10 inches (25 cm) wide and 25 inches (63 cm) long. Cut a face hole in the center of the strip. Fasten the

Carrot

Bacon and Eggs

Hot Dog

Pizza

ends with staples and tape. For the top, make a stiff cap (see page 258). Cover with aluminum foil. For the life pack, connect two cereal boxes like a sandwich board (see Clock). Glue on round plastic bottles and jar lids. Paint the costume silver-gray. **Rocket:** Make a sack costume (see page 257). Glue on pieces of felt or paint the outline of a rocket on the front and back of the sack. Wear a cone crown (see page 259). **Hot Dog:** Make

a sack costume of red felt (see page 257). Glue a piece of gold felt to the sack. Glue on felt relish. **Carrot:** Make a sack costume of orange felt (see page 257). Paint the lines with tempera paint. Glue green felt leaves to the top. **Pizza:** Wear a leotard and tights. Decorate a sandwich board to look like a pizza (see Clock). **Bacon and Eggs:** Wear a leotard and tights. Decorate a sandwich board to look like bacon and eggs (see Clock).

Basic costume

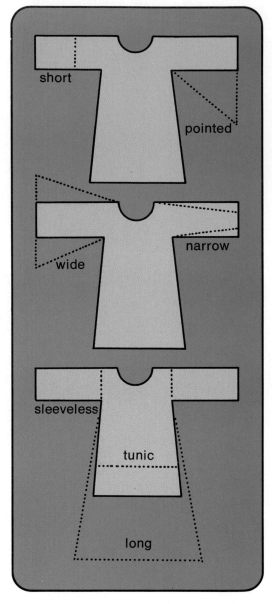

Materials

- bathrobe
- cloth or old sheet
- felt-tip pen
- needle
- newspaper
- scissors
- seam binding (double-fold)
- straight pins
- thread

1 Tape several sheets of newspaper together. Lay your bathrobe on the paper. Trace around the robe, adding 1 inch (2.5 cm) for the seams.

Look at the pictures to see how you can change the basic pattern to make the costume you want.

2 Pin the pattern to a piece of doubled cloth. Cut out the costume.

3 Make a neck opening so you can slip the costume over your head. Cut an 8-inch (20-cm) slit from the neck down the back of the costume.

4 Pin the pieces of cloth together. Sew the shoulder seams, sleeve seams, and side seams (see **backstitch,** page 156). Make 1-inch (2.5 cm) seams.

5 Hem the sleeves and the bottom (see **hemming stitch,** page 156).

Use the backstitch to sew double-fold seam binding around the neck slit and neck. Leave enough seam binding at each end of the neck to make ties. If the costume is sleeveless, sew seam binding around the armholes.

Wear the neck slit in the front or in the back. Turn the flaps under or back, or tie the tie, depending on the costume you are making.

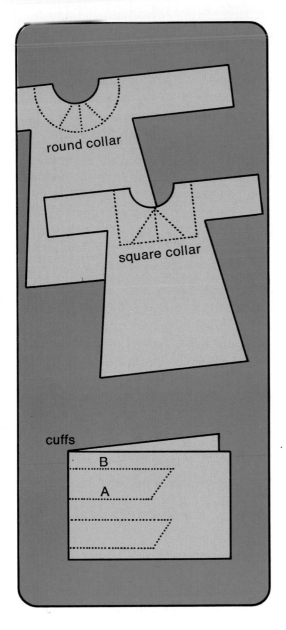

round collar

square collar

cuffs

B

A

Cuffs

To make cuffs, measure the width at the bottom of the sleeve. Draw a line (A) this long on a piece of doubled felt. Draw another line (B) 5 inches (12.5 cm) above the first line. Connect the two lines. Draw another cuff. Cut out the cuffs and sew them to the sleeves (see **backstitch,** page 156).

Sack costume

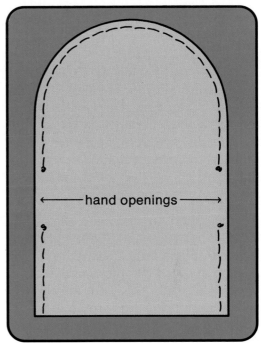

←——— hand openings ———→

1 Fold an old sheet in half and lie down on it. Have someone draw a line around you. Leave an extra 12 inches (30 cm) all around. The shape should look like the one in the picture.

2 Pin around the shape inside the lines. Cut out the shape.

3 Stitch around the shape, leaving an opening on each side for your hands (see **backstitch,** page 156).

4 Cut out eyeholes. Put on the sack and mark the eyeholes with a felt-tip pen. Then take off the sack and cut out the eyeholes.

5 Turn the sack so the seams are inside. Hem the sack (see **hemming stitch,** page 156).

Caps and hats

Soft cap

To make a pattern, measure the distance around your head, plus 1 inch (2.5 cm). Then draw a line half this long on a sheet of paper. Measure up 9 inches (23 cm) from the center of this line and make a mark. Draw a half circle connecting the point and the ends of the line, as shown.

Pin the pattern to a doubled piece of felt. Cut out the shape. Pin the pieces together. Stitch on the dashed line, making a $\frac{1}{2}$-inch (18 mm) seam (see **backstitch,** page 156). Turn the cap so the seam is inside. Turn up the bottom edge of the cap to make a brim about 1 inch (2.5 cm) wide.

Stiff cap

Cut three strips of cardboard, each 2 inches (5 cm) wide and a little longer than the distance around your head. Staple the strips as shown. Cover the frame with foil or glue crepe paper over it.

Brimmed hats

You can make hats with brims and you can make hats with cone, flat, or round crowns. These hats might look difficult to make, but they're really easy. Here's how.

Make the **brim** first. Tape a strip of paper around your head so you know what size to make your hat. Place the taped strip on a large sheet of construction paper. Stretch the strip so it is slightly oval-shaped. Trace around the strip. Draw another line 1 inch (2.5 cm) inside the first line.

Decide how wide you want the brim. Measure this distance from the outside line and draw another line. Cut on this line. Then cut along the inside line (see **inside cuts,** page 37). Cut $\frac{1}{2}$-inch (12-mm) wide slits from the hole up to the line. Fold the flaps up.

For a **cone crown,** draw a quarter-circle with a 16-inch (40-cm) radius. To do this, place your ruler at one corner of a large sheet of construction paper. Make a mark at the 16-inch (40-cm) point. Keep the end of the ruler at the corner of the paper and swing the ruler in an arc. Make more marks. Cut on the curved line. Then tape the straight edges together to make a cone that will fit snugly over the flaps on the brim. Glue the cone to the flaps.

For a **flat crown,** cut a strip of paper long enough to fit around the flaps on the brim and 1 inch (2.5 cm) wider than the height you want the crown. About 1 inch (2.5 cm) from one edge, draw a line down the length of the strip. Cut slits up to the line. Then tape the ends of the strip together so the crown will fit snugly over the brim flaps. Glue the crown to the brim flaps. Fold in the crown flaps and glue on a top.

For a **round crown,** make a stiff cap and glue it to a brim.

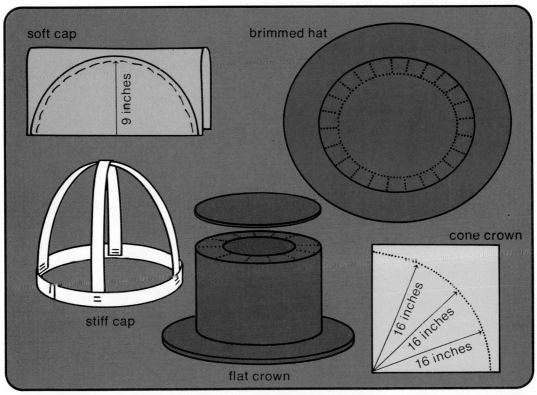

soft cap

9 inches

brimmed hat

stiff cap

flat crown

cone crown

16 inches

16 inches

16 inches

16 inches

Puppets and Plays

Puppets are magical little people. They can do or be whatever you want. Puppets can laugh, cry, jump, or dance. They can be kings or queens or circus clowns.

With you, your puppets can be everything. Without you, they are nothing. They sit in a lump—lifeless little bits of cloth. It's up to you, the puppeteer, to make your puppets come alive.

As the puppeteer, you make the puppets. You make a stage on which they can act. You write the plays for your puppets. And then you turn your puppets into actors on the puppet stage.

So turn the page. Let's get started. You'll find puppets to make, stages to build, and suggestions for plays. As you work with your puppets, they'll tickle your funny bone, tug at your heartstrings, and maybe even give you a great big surprise. It's fun! It's magic! It's the world of "Puppets and Plays"!

Paper puppets

Here are some puppets you can make using just paper and paste. Use your arm for a stage or make a puppet stage (see page 268). And don't forget about the paper-bag puppets on page 28.

Finger puppet

Play with a puppet on your finger. Cut a strip of paper and tape it around your finger. Then slip the paper tube off and press it flat, with the tape on the bottom. Draw a face and color the clothes. Glue on feathers to make an Indian. To make a scary witch, use bits of yarn for crazy hair. Or add ears, whiskers, and a tail to make an animal.

Peppy puppet

Here's a puppet that will dance on your fingers. Draw a picture of a person on stiff cardboard. Draw two big circles instead of legs. Cut out the puppet. Cut out the insides of the circles (see **inside cuts,** page 37). Color the puppet. Put your first and second fingers through the circles. Use your fingers as legs to make your puppet run and play.

Stick puppet

These stick puppets might make you think of lollipops. Draw a picture of a person or an animal on stiff cardboard. Cut out the shape. Glue on, or draw, hair, eyes, nose, mouth, hat, and clothes. Tape a pencil, a plastic drinking straw, or a stick to the back of the puppet to use as a handle. If you want arms and legs that move, cut them out separately and tape them on. Or, punch holes and attach the arms and legs with yarn. Tie on cardboard hands and feet.

Stick-puppet cutout

Cut a strip of cardboard at least 1 inch (2.5 cm) wide and 12 inches (30 cm) long. Score the cardboard three times at each end of the strip (see **scoring,** page 36). Fold on the scores to form a triangle and glue in place. Cut out a magazine picture of a person or animal. It's best if the person or animal is standing. Glue the picture to a stiff piece of cardboard. When the glue is dry, cut out the figure and glue it to the triangle at one end of the strip.

Hand puppets

Hand puppets are easy to make. And there are several ways to make them. With some practice, you'll be able to make these little puppets laugh, cry, ask questions, act surprised, and do many other things that people do.

Sock puppet

Put your hand in an old sock, with the top of your wrist in the sock's heel. To make a mouth, push the toe of the sock between your fingers and your thumb. Ask someone to help you pin the folds at the corners of the mouth. Take off the sock. Sew the pinned corners (see **overcast stitch,** page 156). If you want, you can sew on some red felt for a tongue. Decorate the puppet by sewing on button or felt eyes, felt ears, or yarn hair (see page 267).

Handkerchief puppet

A handkerchief puppet is one of the easiest hand puppets you can make. All you need is a handkerchief or a piece of cloth, a rubber band or a piece of string, and some toilet tissue or cotton balls.

To make the puppet's head, put a small bunch of toilet tissue or cotton balls in the center of a handkerchief. Gather the cloth around the stuffing. Wind a rubber band, or tie a string, around the cloth. Leave the neck loose enough so you can push your first finger into the puppet's head. Cut two small holes in the cloth so you can use your thumb and second finger for the puppet's arms. Draw a face with felt-tip pens and sew on yarn hair (see page 267).

Glove puppet

A glove puppet is a hand puppet with a body that looks like a funny glove. Use the outline on this page to make a pattern for a glove puppet.

Materials

- cloth or felt
- glue (white)
- pencil
- scissors
- tissue paper
- yarn

glue

cut

1 Fold a piece of tissue paper in half. Place the fold along the edge of the page. Trace the outline. Add about 4 inches (10 cm) to the bottom of the pattern. Keep the paper folded and cut along the lines.

2 Open the pattern and pin it to a doubled piece of cloth. Cut out the shape.

3 Glue the two pieces of cloth together with the right sides facing. Place dabs of glue, as shown by the dotted line, on the edges of the top and sides of one cloth piece. Stick the pieces of cloth together. Let the glue dry.

4 Make little cuts along the edge of the cloth, up to the glue line, as shown. Turn the cloth so the right sides are out.

5 Draw a face with felt-tip pens, or use one of the stitches on page 157. Or, glue on pieces of felt. Add yarn hair (see page 267).

6 Stuff the head with toilet tissue or cotton balls. Wind a rubber band or tie a string around the neck. Leave the neck loose enough so you can push your first finger into the head.

Puppet heads

Some glove puppets have separate heads. When you use these puppets, slip your hand into the glove first. Then put on the head.

To make a glove body for these puppet heads, use the pattern on page 265. Instead of making a head, draw a straight neck on the pattern, as shown here. Glue the edges, as shown by the dotted line. Make little cuts up to the glue line, as shown.

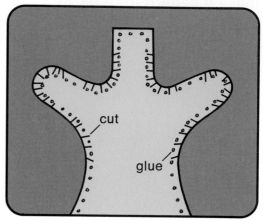

Paper-cup head

Cut a hole about the size of a marble in the side of a paper cup (see **inside cuts,** page 37). This hole will become the nose. Draw or glue on eyes, ears, a mouth, and yarn hair (see page 267). To put on the head, stick your first finger into the cup and through the hole. The end of your finger becomes the nose and helps you hold the head.

Papier-mâché puppet head

You can also turn newspaper into a puppet head. The project on page 98 shows you how.

Styrofoam puppet head

Start with a 3-inch (7.5-cm) Styrofoam ball. You can buy these balls in variety and craft stores. Turn your scissors around and around in the ball to dig a hole that will fit your first finger. Don't dig all the way through the ball.

If you want to make stiff animal ears, push pieces of cardboard into the ball.

Use plain white paper to make strip papier-mâché (see **strip papier-mâché, page 88**). Cover the head, but not the hole, with four layers of strips.

To make the nose, soak tiny pieces of paper in papier-mâché paste. Squeeze the pieces into a lump and stick them to the face. Let dry.

Paint the face with tempera paint (see **tempera paint,** page 66). Paint or glue on eyes and a mouth. Add felt ears and yarn hair (see page 267).

Yarn hair

To make yarn hair, lay a piece of yarn over your puppet's head. Cut it off at the length you want. Then cut twenty to forty pieces of yarn this length. Tie the yarn together in the middle. Put the knot on top of the puppet's head and pin it in place. Glue each strand of hair to the head. Or, sew the knot in place and leave the hair loose. Take out the pin and give your puppet a haircut.

Puppet stages

Puppet stages are made so the audience can see the puppets, but can't see you. Here are some stages you can build with things found around your house.

Chair Stage

Hide behind a big chair or sofa. Use the top of the chair as your stage.

Table Stage

Turn a card table on its side. Hide behind the table top and reach up above the edge to work the puppets. If you want, you can also hang blankets over the legs on each side.

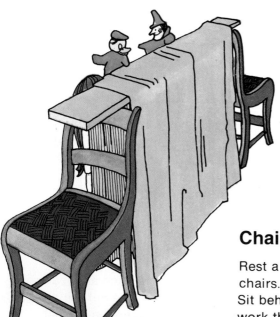

Chairs-and-Board Stage

Rest a board across the backs of two chairs. Hang a blanket over the board. Sit behind the blanket while you work the puppets.

Doorway Stage

Tape a blanket or sheet across the lower part of a doorway. Hide behind the blanket while working the puppets.

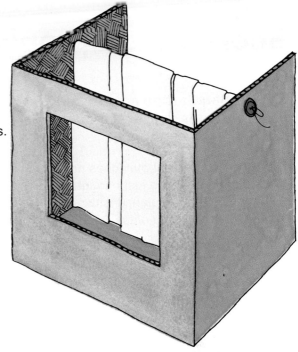

Box Stage

Start with a large box or carton. Cut away one side of the box. To make the front of the stage, cut a window in the other side of the box (see **inside cuts,** page 37). Punch two holes in the sides of the box, near the top. Tie a big button to one end of a long piece of heavy string. Thread the string through the holes, and tie a big button on the other side. Use clip clothespins or safety pins to hang a cloth curtain or a picture from the string. Decorate the front of the stage with tempera paint (see **tempera paint,** page 66). Hang a

blanket over a table and put the stage on it. Stand or sit behind the table and scenery while you work the puppets.

Cardboard Stage

Use a scenery string for this stage just like the one for the box stage.

Scenery and props

Scenery and props help to tell the story your puppets act out.

Scenery for a puppet play does not have to look real. Use just enough scenery to let the audience know where the story takes place.

Paint your scenery on large pieces of paper. Then tack or tape the paper to the wall behind the stage. If you are using a puppet stage with a scenery string, use clothespins or safety pins to hang the scenery from the string.

You can also pin scenery to a stage curtain. Glue magazine pictures to pieces of cardboard. When the glue is dry, cut out the shapes. Then tape an open safety pin, with the point facing down, to the back of the cutout. Pin the cutouts to the curtain.

Props will make your puppets' actions more exciting and more real. If your puppet is going to sweep the floor, he should do it with a broom. For a puppet, a whisk broom is a big, funny broom.

You can also have your puppets brush their teeth with toothbrushes, build make-believe fires with twigs, arrange doll furniture, and hang pictures on the scenery or stage curtain. Puppets can carry fruits and vegetables, pretend to pour liquid from bottles, bake cakes, and write with pencils.

Many of your toys would make good props for your puppet plays.

Choosing and staging puppet plays

What kinds of stories make good puppet plays? Well, it all depends on the people who will see the play, the puppeteers, and the story itself. When you choose a puppet play, ask yourself these three questions.

Who is going to watch the play and what will they like? No matter how young or old the audience is, people like puppets to be very happy or very sad. If a puppet is happy, he should be very, very happy. If a puppet is sad, the audience will like him better if he is very, very sad. And whenever a puppet speaks, he should move about so the audience can tell which puppet is talking.

Different kinds of people like different kinds of stories. But the best puppet plays have only a few characters and tell a very simple story. And the younger the audience, the shorter the play should be.

How many puppets will be on stage at one time? Remember, each puppeteer has only two hands. If you are the only puppeteer, find a play that has no more than two characters on stage at any one time. If you are giving a play with a friend, you can have up to four characters on stage at one time.

Are there enough actions for the puppets to do while they are telling the story? Puppets that just stand still and talk, talk, talk are boring. You'll want to choose a story in which the puppets move about and do things while they're on stage. Any story that has the puppets dance, build houses, sweep floors, sing songs, and act happy, sad, surprised, or frightened makes a good puppet play.

You can turn many of the stories and poems in volumes 1 and 2 of *Childcraft* into puppet plays. Or, you can make up your own puppet plays. Just be sure to have lots of action.

Make a copy of the play for each puppeteer. Underline each person's part with a colored pen or crayon. Then paint the scenery, gather the props, and make the puppets. When everything is ready, call everyone together to practice giving the play. Then when the curtain goes up, you will all know what you're to do and when you are supposed to do it.

Let's Play Games

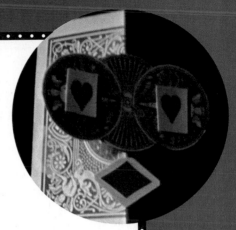

You run as fast as a rabbit. You leap as high as the sky. You spin like a musical merry-go-round. And you laugh! Games are healthy, happy, hearty fun. In this section, you'll find rules for games you can play alone or with the whole gang.

Giving a party? Besides games to play, there are stunts you and your guests can do and magic tricks to amaze and amuse everyone.

There are also outdoor games to play at recess, on the sidewalk in front of your house, or in the backyard.

For quieter times, like rainy days, learn some card games. Play Klondike alone, or other card games with your family and friends.

Indoors, outdoors—rain or shine, what are we waiting for? Let's play games!

Outdoor Games

Captain, May I?

(three or more players)

What's a giant step? How about a banana slip, a scissors, or an umbrella? These are only a few of the steps you can take while playing Captain, May I?

One player is chosen as Captain. The Captain draws a line and faces the other players, who line up on the far side of the yard. The Captain starts the game by calling out a player's name. The Captain tells the player the kind of step to take and how many. He may say, "Susan, you may take two giant steps."

Before the player moves, he or she must ask, "Captain, may I?" The Captain then replies, "Yes, you may," or "No, you may not." If the player moves without asking permission, he or she must go back and start over again.

The first player to cross the line wins and becomes the next Captain.

baby step: Move forward the length of one foot.

backward step: Turn around and take a step backward.

banana slip: Slide one foot forward as far as possible, then draw the other foot up to it.

barrel step: Leap up and spin around, moving forward at the same time.

bunny rabbit: Hop with both feet together.

frog jump: Jump from a crouching position.

giant step: Take as large a step as possible.

scissors step: Jump forward and land with feet apart; take a second jump and land with feet together.

soldier step: Step forward with your legs stiff.

umbrella step: Twirl around on one foot with arms stretched out. As you complete the turn, step forward with your other foot.

Outdoor Games

Statues

(three or more players)

Draw a line on the ground or pavement. Draw another line some distance away. The players stand on one line. Whoever is "It" stands on the other line. The idea of the game is to see which player can reach the other side first.

The player who is "It" turns his back and counts aloud to ten. As he counts, the other players walk or run toward him. At the count of ten, "It" whirls around. The others stop and freeze into statues. Any player caught moving must go back to the starting line. The one who is "It" can count as slowly or as fast as he wants. He can also start to count slowly and then speed up, or start to count quickly and then slow down.

This goes on until one player crosses the line and wins the game. The winner is now "It" and the game starts again.

Duck, Duck, Goose

(ten or more players)

In this chasing game, the player who is "It" is the Goose. The other players are Ducks. They squat in a circle.

To start the game, Goose walks around the outside of the circle, touching each player on the head. Each time Goose touches a player, Goose says, "Duck." But if Goose touches a player's head and says "Goose," the fun begins.

That player jumps up and chases Goose around the circle. If Goose reaches the player's place before being tagged, the player becomes the next Goose. But if Goose is tagged, Goose is "It" again.

Tom Tiddler's Ground

(five or more players)

Draw a straight line or a large circle on the ground. The player who is Tom Tiddler stands on one side of the line or inside the circle. The other players stand on the other side of the line or outside the circle.

The players tease Tom by crossing over the line or into the circle. They add to the teasing by chanting:

I'm on Tom Tiddler's ground,
Picking up gold and silver!

Then they run back to safety before Tom tags them. If tagged, that player becomes Tom Tiddler and the game continues.

Outdoor Games

Fox and Geese

(ten or more players)

Choose one player to be the Fox and another to be the Gander. The other players become the Geese.

To start the game, the Geese line up behind the Gander. The first Goose places his hands on the shoulders of the Gander. The other Geese place their hands on the shoulders of the players in front of them. The Gander tries to keep the last player in line from being caught by the Fox.

The Fox tries to tag the last Goose. To keep the Fox from doing this, the Gander runs, dodges, twists, and turns. The Geese follow the Gander, keeping their hands on the shoulders of the players in front of them. But they can also twist and turn to help the Gander protect the end player from being tagged by the Fox.

When the Fox tags the last Goose, that player becomes the Fox and the Fox becomes the Gander. The game is usually played until every Goose gets a chance to be both Fox and Gander.

Indoor or Outdoor Games

Rock, Scissors, Paper

(two players)

This game is played with three simple hand signs: a fist for a rock, two fingers in a V-shape for scissors, and an open hand for paper.

To start, the players hide their hands behind their backs and count aloud to three. At the count of three, they each put out a hand and make a sign.

If both players make the same sign, there is no score. But if the signs are different, a point is scored in this way: rock wins over scissors because rock can break scissors; scissors wins over paper because scissors can cut paper; and paper wins over rock because paper can cover rock. You can play for any number of points.

Indoor or Outdoor Games

Sardines

(five or more players)

One player leaves the room and hides. While he is hiding, the others count aloud to 50. Then everyone looks for the hidden player.

Anyone who finds the hidden player quietly joins him or her in the hiding place. One by one, the players are squeezed together until they are packed like sardines in a can.

Drop the Handkerchief

(six or more players)

One player is "It." The others join hands and form a circle. They then sit down and put their hands behind them. The player who is "It" has a handkerchief and skips around the circle as everybody sings:

A tisket, a tasket,
A green and yellow basket,
I sent a letter to my love
And on the way I dropped it,
I dropped it, I dropped it.

"It" drops the handkerchief into a player's hands and starts to run. The player must run in the opposite direction. The first to reach the empty place sits down. The other player is "It."

Pussy Wants a Corner

(five players)

Pussy stands in the middle of the room or yard. The other players stand in a corner or other spot.

The player who is "It" goes from player to player asking for a corner. He is always told to see a neighbor. While this is going on, the corner players call to each other and try to exchange places before Pussy can reach an empty corner. The player who winds up without a corner becomes Pussy. Pussy can also stand in the middle and call, "Everybody change!" Then all the players must change corners, giving Pussy a chance to get one of the corners.

Jack and Jill

(ten or more players)

Choose a boy to be Jack and a girl to be Jill. The other players join hands and form a circle around them.

Jack is blindfolded with a handkerchief. He calls out, "Where are you, Jill?" and tries to tag her. Jill must answer him. But she keeps ducking to keep from being tagged.

When Jack does tag Jill, he takes off the blindfold and joins the circle. Jill picks another Jack from the circle. This time, Jill is blindfolded and tries to tag Jack. When she calls, "Where are you, Jack?" he must answer. After Jill tags Jack, she gives him the blindfold and joins the circle. Before he's blindfolded, Jack picks a new Jill and the game starts all over again.

Indoor or Outdoor Games

London Bridge

(six or more players)

Two players are chosen to form the bridge. Each "bridge" player picks a symbol that will represent him—a rose, a ring, or anything else. These two players then join hands and hold them up as high as they can. This is the "bridge" the other players go under in single file. As the players circle around and around, under the "bridge," they sing:

> London Bridge is falling down,
> Falling down, falling down,
> London Bridge is falling down,
> My fair lady.

On the words, "my fair lady," the "bridge" drops and locks in a player. Still holding hands, the "bridge" players swing the "fair lady" back and forth as they sing:

> Take the keys and lock her up,
> Lock her up, lock her up,
> Take the keys and lock her up,
> My fair lady.

The captured player is taken aside and asked to choose between the two symbols that represent the "bridge" players. The prisoner then stands behind the "bridge" player of his choice, with his hands around that person's waist.

The game continues until all players have been captured. The two teams now have a tug of war to see which one is the winner.

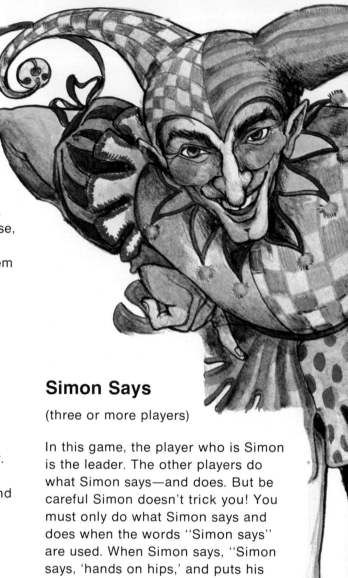

Simon Says

(three or more players)

In this game, the player who is Simon is the leader. The other players do what Simon says—and does. But be careful Simon doesn't trick you! You must only do what Simon says and does when the words "Simon says" are used. When Simon says, "Simon says, 'hands on hips,' and puts his hands on his hips, the players must

do this, too. But if Simon just says, "Hands on hips"—without first saying "Simon says,"—don't do it! If you do, you're out.

Simon can trick you another way. Simon can give an order to do one thing but do another. For example, suppose Simon says, "Simon says, 'hands on hips'" but claps his hands instead. If you clap your hands, you've been tricked and you're out! The last player becomes Simon in the next game.

The Farmer in the Dell

(eight or more players)

One player is chosen to be the farmer. The others join hands and form a circle around the farmer. They then skip around the farmer, singing:

> The farmer in the dell,
> The farmer in the dell,
> Heigh-ho, the derry-o,
> The farmer in the dell.

The farmer picks a player to be the wife. This player joins the farmer in the circle. The others continue to skip around them, singing:

> The farmer takes a wife,
> The farmer takes a wife,
> Heigh-ho, the derry-o,
> The farmer takes a wife.

After each verse, the last player to enter the circle selects the next player to come in. The remaining verses are: the wife picks a child . . . the child picks a nurse . . . the nurse picks a dog . . . the dog picks a cat . . . the cat picks a rat . . . the rat picks the cheese.

When the cheese is chosen, all players clap their hands and skip around the cheese, singing:

> The cheese stands alone,
> The cheese stands alone,
> Heigh-ho, the derry-o,
> The cheese stands alone.

The cheese becomes the farmer if the game is played again.

Indoor or Outdoor Games

Musical Chairs

(six or more players)

This game, also known as Going to Jerusalem, is a good party game. All you need to play this game are some chairs and music. For the music you can use a record player, a radio, or a musical instrument. One person is put in charge of the music. This person starts and stops the music as the others play the game.

Set the chairs in a row. Arrange them so that they face in opposite directions, as shown. You will need chairs for all but one of the players.

When the music starts, the players march around and around the chairs. Suddenly, the music stops. Then the players scramble to sit down on the chairs. One player will be left standing. This player is out of the game and takes away one chair. The music starts again and the game continues. After each scramble for chairs, the player left standing removes a chair. Finally, only one chair and two players are left. The player who gets the chair wins.

Follow the Leader

(five or more players)

In this lively game, the Leader can jump, dance, make faces, turn a somersault—just about any action he or she wants the other players to do.

The other players follow the Leader in single file and imitate everything the Leader does. Any player who misses is out of the game. This goes on until there's only one follower. Then he or she becomes the next Leader.

Hot Potato

(ten or more players)

A ball, some crumpled paper, or a beanbag is the "hot potato" in this lively game.

Choose one player to be "It." The other players sit in a circle on the floor or on the ground, with "It" in the middle.

"It" starts the game by tossing the "hot potato" to a player. The players then toss the "hot potato" back and forth across the circle, while "It" tries to catch it. If a player misses a catch or drops the "hot potato," he or she changes places with "It." And if "It" catches the "hot potato," the player who tossed it is "It."

Dog and Bone

(ten or more players)

This is a game in which the players try to take away Dog's bone without Dog knowing it. The player who is "It" is Dog. The bone can be a key, a spoon, an eraser, or any other small object.

Dog sits on a chair with his eyes closed. The "bone" is under the chair. The players sit in a circle around Dog. One person—a grown-up or the oldest player in the group—acts as leader and stands outside the circle of players. The leader points to one of the players. This player tries to sneak up, steal the bone, and get back to his place without Dog hearing him.

If Dog hears the player, he barks. The player then goes back to his place. The leader points to another player who tries to get the bone. This continues until a player is successful. Then all the players put their hands behind their backs. Dog is told to open his eyes and guess who has the bone.

Dog gets three chances to guess who has the bone. If he guesses correctly, the player with the bone becomes Dog. If Dog fails to guess, he is out of the game. The leader then picks another player to be Dog.

Card Games

ABC's of Card Playing

Card games are lots of fun. But to play, you have to know the names of the cards and the value of each one. There are also special words and rules to learn.

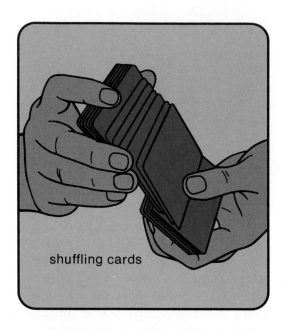
shuffling cards

A **deck** or **pack** has 52 cards made up of four suits. The **suits**—spades, hearts, diamonds, and clubs—are shown by markings on the cards. There are 13 cards in each suit. From lowest to highest, these usually are: ace, 2, 3, 4, 5, 6, 7, 8, 9, 10, jack, queen, and king. The ace, however, is a special card. It can be low, high, or both, depending on the game you're playing.

To begin a game with two or more players, you must find out who goes first or who deals the cards. Spread the cards out, facedown. Each player takes one card. The player with the highest card goes first or is the dealer.

The **dealer** hands out the cards to the other players. Before play begins, the dealer **shuffles**, or mixes, the cards.

The cards are then **cut** by the player on the dealer's right. He takes five or more cards from the top of the deck and puts them on the bottom.

The **deal** is the handing out of the cards. Usually, the cards are dealt one at a time. The dealer gives the first card to the player on his left, and so on around the group until all players have the number of cards they need.

cutting cards

The **stock** consists of a pile of any cards left over after a deal. Players take cards from the stock according to the rules of the game being played.

A **pair** is two cards having the same value, such as two 4's.

Three or four of a kind is three or four cards having the same value, such as three 9's or four jacks.

club

diamond

heart

spade

A♠

ace

king

K♠

Q♠

queen

jack

J♠

Card Games

Concentration

(two to six players)

Shuffle the cards and spread them facedown on the table. You may arrange the cards in rows, but it's more fun to just scatter them around any old way.

Each player, in turn, turns up any two cards, one at a time, so everyone can see them. If the cards have the same value, the player keeps them and draws two more. As long as he draws pairs, he continues to play. When he draws two cards that don't match, the player puts them back, facedown, exactly where he got them.

Everyone then concentrates and tries to remember where these cards are. The skill is in remembering where to find matching cards when it is your turn. This is why the game is called concentration.

The game continues until all the cards have been paired. The player who has the most pairs of cards is the winner.

I Doubt It

(three to five players)

Deal all the cards. Some players may get more cards than others. This does not matter. The player to the left of the dealer starts. He puts one, two, three, or four cards facedown on the table. He then says they are all aces, the high card. What he says may or may not be true.

Any one of the other players may say, ''I doubt it,'' and look at the cards. If the first player was bluffing, he loses and must take back his cards.

The next player, in turn, puts down one to four cards and says they are kings. If nobody doubts it, the cards stay facedown on the table. From then on, any player who loses must pick up all cards on the table.

Players, in turn, name the card of the next highest value—queens, jacks, tens, all the way down to twos. Then they start again with aces.

The player who gets rid of all his cards is the winner.

Klondike

(one player)

This is a game of solitaire, which means you play it alone. Shuffle a deck of cards. Then, deal out seven cards in a row. The first card should be faceup, the other six facedown. Next, deal out six more cards on top of the row of facedown cards. Again, the first card should be faceup. Continue doing this until you have seven cards in the last pile. The top card in each pile should be faceup.

Keep the rest of the cards facedown, to be used as stock (see **stock**, page 286). If there are any aces among the faceup cards, put them above your layout, faceup. Every time you take a faceup card from a pile, you turn over the next card in that pile. The ace has a value of 1. You build cards of the same suit on the ace, starting with the 2 and continuing up to the king.

The faceup card or cards are now moved from pile to pile. When you move a faceup card or cards to another pile, it must be put on top of a higher card of a different color. For example, you put a red 9 on a black 10.

If you remove an entire pile, you can put a king in the empty space and start building down from it.

The leftover cards, or stock, are turned over, one by one. Those that can be used are added to the piles. Aces are placed above the layout, where they are built on. The unused cards are turned over again and again, until they are all used up, or until there are no more possible plays. You win when you have built up to the king on all the aces.

Go Fish

(two to five players)

If there are two players, each one gets seven cards. If there are more than two players, each one gets five cards. The leftover cards are placed in the middle of the table for "fishing."

The player to the left of the dealer goes first. He asks any player for cards that will match the value of a card or cards he has in his hand. For example, if he has one or more aces, he asks, "Do you have any aces?" The player who was asked must give up any aces he has. As long as the first player gets what he asked for, he continues to play. When he gets four of a kind, he puts these cards down in front of him.

When a player is asked for a card he does not have, he says, "Go fish." The first player then picks up the top card from the pile in the middle of the table. If this gives him four of a kind, he puts these cards down in front of him. If not, he adds the card to his hand. In either case, this completes his turn.

The player to the left goes next. The game goes on till a player matches all his cards and has none left in his hand. This player is the winner.

Pencil and Paper Games

Tick-Tack-Toe

(two players)

This simple game is also known as Tit-Tat-Toe and Naughts and Crosses.

Draw two lines down and two lines across to make nine spaces. Onc player uses an X to mark spaces. The other player uses an O.

The idea is to get three of your marks in a row—across, up and down, or on a slant. But you must also be careful to block the other player. The first player to get three of his marks in a row draws a line through his marks. He is the winner. The loser gets to go first in the next game. This game often ends in a tie. When this happens, take turns going first.

Boxes

(two or more players)

On a piece of paper, draw five or more rows of dots, as shown. Each player, in turn, draws a line to connect two dots. The line must go up and down or across—never on a slant.

A player who closes a box writes his initial in the box and gets another turn. If he cannot close a box, he looks for a place to draw a line that will not help another player. When all the boxes are closed, the player with the most boxes wins the game.

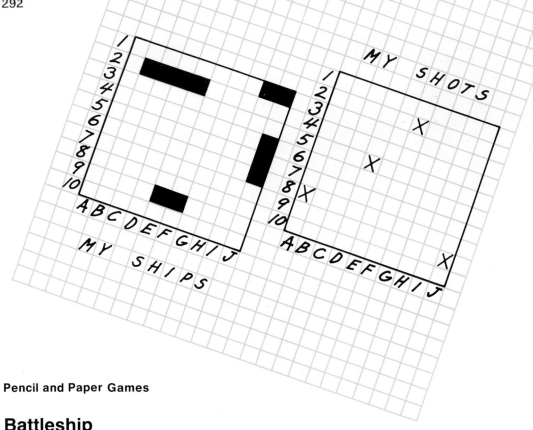

Pencil and Paper Games

Battleship

(two players)

To play this game, each player needs a pencil and a sheet of graph paper—the kind with little squares. Each player draws two boxes with numbers and letters, as shown. The box on the left is for your ships. The other is to keep track of your shots.

Each player starts with one battleship, one cruiser, and two destroyers. Use four squares for the battleship, three for the cruiser, and two for each destroyer, as shown. Mark your ships anywhere inside the left-hand box. Just be sure the ships do not touch one another. And don't let the other player see your paper!

You are ready to shoot. You are allowed·four shots, one for each ship. Try to imagine where your opponent has placed his ships. To fire a shot,

call out the number and letter of a square. For example, 8-A. Your other three shots might be 5-D, 2-F, and 9-J. In the box on the right, put an X in the square as you call a shot.

After you've fired all four shots, your opponent tells you how many hits you scored. He also tells you what kind of ship or ships you hit. But he does not tell you which of your shots were hits. Then it's his turn to fire four shots, and you tell him what happened.

To sink a ship, you must score a hit on every square occupied by the ship. When a player's ship has been sunk, he must say so. Each time one of your ships is sunk, you get one less shot on your next turn. The first player to sink all the enemy's ships wins the battle.

Nine Men's Morris

(two players)

This game calls for a special board. You can draw the design for the board on a piece of cardboard about the size of a checkerboard. Or, you can make a wooden board following the instructions on page 237.

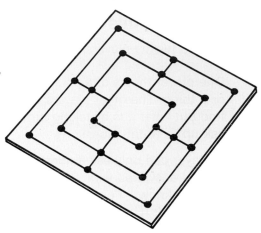

For the counters, or men, use bottle caps, buttons, checkers, or coins. If you make the wooden board, you should use golf tees for the men. You will need nine men of one color and nine of another color.

Each player starts with nine men. The idea of the game is to capture seven of the other player's men. The first player to do this wins.

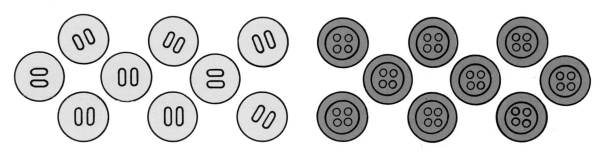

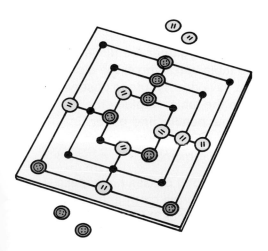

To begin, the players take turns placing their men on the circles. Only one man may be placed on each circle. Each player tries to get three men in a row, and also keep the other from doing this. A row of men may be either up and down or across. If a player gets three of his men in a row, he takes one of the other player's men.

When all the men are on the board, the players take turns moving the men. The men are always moved along a line to the next circle. The object is still to get three of your men in a row and keep the other player from doing this.

Each time a player gets three men in a row, he or she takes any one of the other player's men that isn't in a row of three. When a player has only three men left, he may move a man anywhere on the board. A player wins when the other player has only two men left.

Guessing Games

Twenty Questions

(two to twenty players)

One player thinks of a person, a place, or a thing. The other players try to find out what it is by taking turns to ask up to twenty questions.

A player can only ask a question that can be answered with "Yes," "No," or "I don't know." For example, a player can ask, "Is it bigger than a breadbox?" But a player can't ask, "How big is it?"

The player who guesses the correct answer before twenty questions are used up becomes the next player to choose a person, place, or thing. Otherwise, the first player tells the answer and gets another turn.

Observation

(two or more players)

Before the game, place ten to twenty different things on a table. Cover them with a cloth. The more things you use, the harder—and more challenging—the game will be.

The things should be large enough to be seen easily—such as an acorn, a button, a crayon, a dish, an egg, a fountain pen, a glove, a harmonica, an ice-cream cone, and a hairbrush.

To start the game, gather the players around the table and remove the cloth. The players have one minute to observe the items on the table. Replace the cloth. Hand out pencils and paper. Give the players five minutes to list things they can remember.

Time's up! Each one passes his paper to the left. Remove the cloth and have the players check the list.

Score one point for each correct answer. But take away two points for any item on a list that's not on the table. The player with the highest score wins the game.

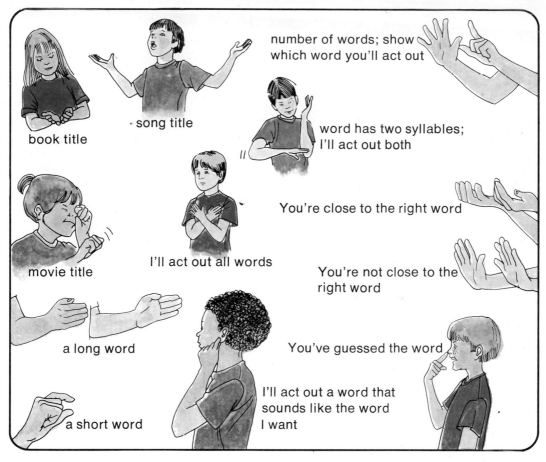

book title

song title

number of words; show which word you'll act out

word has two syllables; I'll act out both

You're close to the right word

I'll act out all words

movie title

You're not close to the right word

a long word

You've guessed the word

a short word

I'll act out a word that sounds like the word I want

Charades

(four or more players)

Charades is a game in which you act out a word or group of words. This popular party game is the most fun when it's played by two teams. Team 1 leaves the room while Team 2 remains. Each team decides on a category, such as titles of books, songs, or movies.

On a slip of paper, each player writes a title in the category picked. The slips are folded so the other team can't see what's written on them. The teams come together and the action begins.

A member of Team 1 picks a slip from Team 2. He then acts out the category and the words written on the slip. The actor must not speak, but he can shake his head "yes" or "no" to answer questions and guesses from teammates. He may act out the words any way he wants to. By using the standard signs shown in the pictures, a great deal of time can be saved.

Teammates have five minutes to guess all the words in the title being acted out. The other team keeps track of the time with an egg timer or watch.

If they guess the title before time's up, the team scores a point. Otherwise, there's no score and a member of Team 2 draws a slip from Team 1. This continues until each player gets a chance to act out a title. The team with the most points is the winner.

Come to My Party

Everyone has a birthday, and the best way to celebrate a birthday is with a party! But, you don't have to wait for your birthday to give a party. You can have one any day of the year.

Do you know how many different kinds of parties you can have? And when is the best time to have a party? And how to invite your guests? And do you know how to plan a party that will make your guests say "That was a great party! When are you going to give another one?"

To answer these and other questions, turn the page and find out how to give the best party ever!

What kind of party?

Start by thinking about the kind of party you'd like to have. Then you can make all your plans for invitations, decorations, refreshments, and games around that idea, or theme.

There are lots of times when you can have a party. You can have a birthday party, a hello or going-away party, and a start- or end-of-school party. How about a party to celebrate a special holiday or to welcome a new season?

You'll probably think of many other times when you might give a party.

You can also combine a special occasion party with a special party idea. If your birthday falls near a holiday, you might want to plan your birthday party around the holiday. If the circus is in town, you might have a circus party at home or going-places birthday party at the circus.

More party ideas

barbecue party

comic strip characters party (guests come dressed as comic strip characters)

cowboys and Indians, or pirates party

going-places party (go to the zoo, a museum, a movie, or a ball game)

hobo party

make-and-do party (everyone makes a craft project at the party)

Mother Goose party

picnic party

skating party

sledding party

storybook party (guests come dressed as storybook characters)

swimming party

trains or planes party

when-I-grow-up party (everyone comes dressed as what they want to be when they grow up)

	Ages of Guests									
	3	**4**	**5**	**6**	**7**	**8**	**9**	**10**	**11**	**12**
Lunch Party	10:30-12:30 or 12:00-2:00			12:00-2:30 or 12:30-3:00 or 1:00-3:30						
Afternoon Party (snacks only)	3:00-4:30*						2:00-4:30 or 3:00-5:30*			
Dinner Party	3:30-5:30*						3:30-6:00 or 4:00-6:30*			
Evening Party (snacks only)								7:00-9:00 or 9:30		

*Plan wintertime parties so everyone will be home before dark.

When should I have my party?

When you plan a party, you should pick a day when most of your guests will be able to come. You should also set a time limit so that no one will get tired and cranky before the party ends.

Weekends and holidays are the best party days. None of your guests will be tired after a busy day at school. And most children will have someone at home who can take them to the party and pick them up when it is over.

Most guests are very excited about coming to a party. They often arrive early. And sometimes, parents are late picking up their children afterward. So, most parties usually last a little longer than planned. Always plan a few extra activities for those who come early or leave late.

Whom will I invite?

Should I invite my whole class to the party? What about my cousins? And my brothers and sisters and their friends? What about the children next door or the children of my parents' friends? The answers to these and other questions will depend upon a number of things, such as your age, where you are having the party, and, of course, the wishes of your parents.

Before you make a guest list, you should decide how many children to invite. A good rule is to invite one or two guests for each candle on your birthday cake. And remember to count yourself as a guest. Of course, the exact number of guests you invite will depend on the kind of party you're giving, if the party is inside or outside, and if your guests are active or quiet.

You'll also need a few grown-ups to help. It's a good idea to invite one grown-up for every four guests. The older your guests, the less grown-up help you'll need.

The guests should be your friends. It seems that at the best parties, the guests always know one another. If your playmates and school chums happen to be your cousins or your brothers and sisters and their friends, then invite them. Otherwise, stick to the boys and girls you play with.

How do I invite my guests?

Inviting your guests is the first part of all the excitement and fun that is to come.

A written invitation is the best kind of invitation. This way, all your guests will have the right information about your party. And they can save the invitation as a reminder of the party festivities.

Half the fun of any party is making the invitations. If you've decided on a special theme for your party, you can plan your invitations around that idea.

Send your invitations about ten days before the party. If you send them too early, people may mislay them or forget about the party. On the other hand, if you send the invitations too late, some of your guests may not be able to come. You can either mail your invitations or pass them out in person.

What about decorations?

Decorations add to the party feeling. You can make decorations for the party room and table that will help you carry out the party idea, or theme.

Streamers and balloons are good decorations for any party. You can buy crepe-paper streamers in a variety store, or you can make paper chains (see page 17). Hang your streamers or chains from the ceiling, window and door frames, and banisters. Then blow up lots of balloons and tie strings to the necks. Rub the balloons against your clothes. Then stick the balloons to the walls and ceiling. When the party is over, you can give each guest a balloon to take home.

Refreshments are an important part of any party. So you'll want to **decorate the table.**

Cover the table with a gaily colored paper tablecloth. You can buy paper tablecloths with pictures printed on them. Or, you can tape party theme cutouts to a plain tablecloth. Set each place with paper plates, cups, and napkins.

And don't forget to make a **table centerpiece** that will help carry out your party theme. You could make a big candy cutie (see page 223), but use lollipops instead of wrapped candies. Or, glue theme cutouts on straws and stick the straws into a styrofoam base. Or, you might want to try a fairy-tale cookie castle (see page 304). If you're having a train party, you could make a shoebox train (see page 24) and fill it with popcorn, candy, or small favors.

All your guests will be happy if you put a small favor at each one's place. A favor is a tiny toy your guest can play with at the table and take home when the party is over.

If you have lots of toilet-paper tubes, you can make super favors. For each guest, fill a tube with peanuts, candies, pennies, and tiny toys. Tape both ends closed and wrap the tube with gift-wrapping paper.

Or, you can put favors in a **Jack Horner Pie** and use the pie for a table decoration. Wrap the favors and tie a long streamer to each one. Put the favors into a large basket or carton. Decorate it to look like a pie. Tape on a paper top, with all the streamers coming out. Each guest takes a streamer and pulls out a favor.

Take-home bags will help all your guests carry home their prizes, candies, and favors after the party.

Decorate plain paper lunch bags around the party theme and print a guest's name on each bag. Or, have your guests decorate their own bags before the start of the party.

What will we eat?

A party means refreshments! What you eat at the party depends on the party time (see page 299). You may serve a meal, or you may serve only snacks. Whatever you plan, you can turn ordinary foods into specialties that will fit in with your party theme.

Sweets

Start off your refreshments with a sweet. Decorate each place setting with a tiny party basket filled with nuts and candies. Or, build animals and people with marshmallows, gumdrops, and toothpicks.

Ice Cream and Cake

A party isn't a party without ice cream and cake. Here are some special ways you can serve them.

Circus Clown Put a scoop of ice cream in an ice-cream cone. Turn the cone upside down on a plate. Use chocolate chips or gumdrops to make the face on the ice cream.

Flowerpot Fill a paper cup with ice cream. Stick in a lollipop for a flower.

Frosty the Snowman Stack two scoops of vanilla ice cream on a plate. Sprinkle on coconut. Add a gumdrop hat and chocolate-chip eyes, nose, and mouth.

Jack-o'-Lantern Put a scoop of orange sherbet on a plate. Stick a candle in the top and add chocolate chips or gumdrops for the eyes, nose, and mouth.

Make-Your-Own-Sundaes Older boys and girls enjoy making their own

sundaes. All you have to do is put the plates and ingredients on a side table.

Circus Cupcake Stand an animal cracker on top of an iced cupcake. Stick three straws into the cupcake and use icing to glue a cookie on top of the straws.

Spring Basket Cupcakes Push a pipe cleaner into a cupcake to make a handle. Then add gumdrop flowers.

Fairy-Tale Cookie Castle Make a cardboard house for a base. Then spread cake icing over the house and stick cookies into the icing (see

picture on page 302). Pull off the cookies and eat them with the ice cream.

Drinks

You can give your party drinks a festive air, too. Serve punch in a color that goes with the party theme. For example, serve orangeade at a Halloween party and strawberry soda pop at a Valentine's party. Make fancy ice cubes by freezing some of your punch. Or, push a cherry or strawberry into each cube before you freeze it. Slip a party theme cutout on each straw.

Meals

If you're serving a meal, you can make party-perfect sandwiches in all kinds of special shapes. Use cookie cutters to cut the bread into different shapes. Or, you might want to serve pizzas or hamburgers from the local drive-in. Of course, hot dogs are terrific at any mealtime party.

But remember, most boys and girls don't like to eat strange foods. So try to serve foods all the children will like. Save your more unusual favorites for another day.

What will we do?

Now that you've chosen your party idea and have sent the invitations, it's time to plan the party activities. Planning what's going to happen and when will help to make your party a success.

Some guests will arrive early. Others will be late. Plan to keep early arrivals busy for about half an hour before the party is due to start. You can play games, color, or put puzzles together.

Having a make-and-do party hat table is one of the best ways to fill this time. Set a table with paper plates and bags, construction paper, string, yarn, glue, scissors, crayons, and odds and ends. As your guests arrive, greet them, help them with their coats and hats, and show them to the make-and-do table. Let each guest make his or her own party hat. Later, you can all decide who has the prettiest hat, the funniest hat, and so on.

If you receive presents at your party, everyone will be curious about what is in the packages. Plan to spend about ten or fifteen minutes opening presents as soon as all the guests have finished making their hats, pictures, or puzzles.

Refreshments are an important part of any party. Allow about half an hour for a meal and twenty minutes for snacks.

Plan to spend the rest of the party playing games (see pages 274-295). During a two-hour party, you can play about nine games. When you plan the games, be sure to mix active and quiet games. And be especially sure to plan a quiet game for just before and after the refreshments. Whenever you can, try to make the games carry out your party theme. And although it's not a game, everyone enjoys hearing a good story read aloud.

You should write down your party plan and be ready with a few extra games just in case the party moves more quickly than you thought it would.

Whenever you plan a going-places party, be sure to purchase tickets and arrange for transportation well in advance. It's also a good idea to arrange for extra grown-up help and to pair off the guests so no one is left alone or lost during the trip.

Henry's Fourth Birthday

Lunch Party 10:30 to 12:30

10:30 to 11:00

draw and color

play with puzzles

play with Henry's toys

11:00 to 11:15

open gifts

11:15 to 11:45

games

    Duck, Duck, Goose

    London Bridge

    Egg-Carton Race

    Treasure Hunt (string beads)

    Farmer in the Dell

story

11:45 to 12:15

lunch

12:15 to 12:30

Treasure Hunt (candy)

get ready to go home

Extra Games: Simon Says, Dog and Bone

    Sailboat Race

Katy's Halloween Party (8 years old)

Afternoon Party 3:00 to 5:30

3:00 to 3:30

Make-and-Do Halloween masks

3:30 to 3:45

guess who's behind the masks

judge the masks

3:45 to 4:15

games

    Pass the Orange

    Pin the Hat on the Witch

    Tin-Can Toss

    Bingo (use the words, "I met an old

      spook who was a witch")

    Bob for Apples

scary story

4:15 to 4:45

refreshments

4:45 to 5:15

trick-or-treat around the block

    (grown-up help)

5:15 to 5:30

meet back at Katy's to collect prizes

    and get ready to go home

Al's Going-Places Party (11 years old)

Afternoon Party 12:00 to 4:30

12:00 to 12:30

open gifts as guests arrive

Make-and-Do name tags (everyone makes

    a name tag that shows his name and

    Al's name, address, and telephone

    number)

12:30 to 1:00

drive to the circus

look for out-of-state license plates

1:00 to 4:00

enjoy the circus

refreshments purchased at the circus

4:00 to 4:30

drive home

give out favors

get ready to go home

Party Games

Everyone enjoys party games. Here are some you can play at your party. The ages are only a suggestion. Many older boys and girls still enjoy games suggested for younger children.

Telephone (ages 9-12)

This game can be played around the party table. One guest whispers a message to the person on his or her right. This person passes on the message. The last one to receive the message tells it out loud. Is it the same message that was started?

Treasure Hunt (ages 3-8)

Hide candy all around the party room. Tell the guests to find as many pieces of candy as they can. You can hide colored eggs at Easter and candy canes at Christmas. Or, you can hide beads and then let everyone string their beads.

Pin the Tail on the Donkey

(all ages)

Hang a big picture of a donkey on the wall. Give each guest a numbered tail with a piece of masking tape on the end. One at a time, blindfold and spin each guest around three times. Then face the person toward the wall. Each one then walks to the wall and tries to pin the tail on the donkey. The one whose tail comes closest to the right spot wins the game. Or, pin hats on witches, stars on Christmas trees, or noses on clowns.

Pass the Orange (ages 9-12)

Everyone stands in a circle. You hold an orange under your chin and try to pass it to the person on your right. The person on your right tries to take the orange under his chin. No one may use their hands during this game. Any player who drops the orange is out.

Spoon Race (all ages)

Give each guest a spoon and a cup with fifty beans in it. The guests put their cups behind the starting line. They must use the spoon to move all the beans to an empty cup behind the finish line. Each guest can carry as many beans and make as many trips as he wants. The first one to move all his beans to the finish line wins the game. It's a good idea to print each guest's name on his or her cup.

Potato Race (ages 9-12)

Give each guest a potato. Everyone must walk from the start to the finish line with the potato on the toe of his shoe. If the potato falls off, it may be put back. The first one to cross the finish line wins the game. Or, play this game as a relay race. Give a potato to each team.

Bingo (ages 3-8)

Have all the guests sit in a circle. A ball is passed around the circle while everyone sings this song:

> I knew an old farmer who had a dog
>   And Bingo was his name.
> B-I-N-G-O, B-I-N-G-O, B-I-N-G-O,
>   And Bingo was his name.

The one who has the ball when the song ends is out. Start over again. Keep going until one player is left. That player is the winner!

More Party Games

Here are more party games you will find on other pages in this book.

Ages 3-8		Ages 9-12		All Ages	
Dog and Bone	285	Boxes	291	Duck, Duck, Goose	277
Egg-Carton Race	32	Charades	295	Musical Chairs	284
Farmer in the Dell	283	Observation	294	Simon Says	282
London Bridge	282			Tiddlywinks	32
Sailboat Race	33			Tin-Can Toss	32

What about prizes?

Winning prizes is fun, but guests who don't win a prize may be very disappointed. Here are some ways to let everyone win a prize or a "thank-you-for-coming" favor.

Winning Stars

Give the guests cards with their name on them. After each game, award four stars for first place, three stars for second place, two stars for third place, and one star to everyone else. When the games are over, set out unwrapped prizes, one for each person. The guest with the most stars gets first choice, and so on. The host or hostess takes the last prize.

Jack Horner Pie

Wrap a prize for each guest. Put the prizes in a big Jack Horner Pie (see page 303). When the party is over, each guest pulls out a "thank-you-for-coming" favor.

Piñata

Make a piñata (see page 102) and fill it with candy or small party favors. Hang the piñata from the ceiling or from the limb of a tree. Everyone stands in a big circle under the piñata. Blindfold one person, give him or her a big stick, and spin him or her around and around. That person has one minute to knock the piñata down. If he or she fails, another guest tries. When someone knocks the piñata down, divide the candy or favors among the children.

The party-planner's check list

Here's a check list that will help you have a successful party. It tells you what to do and when to do it.

Before the Party

Two Weeks Before

ask your parents for permission to have a party

decide on the date and the time

decide on the theme, guests, activities, and refreshments

make the invitations

Ten Days Before

send the invitations

plan the favors, decorations, and prizes

plan the activities and refreshments

start to practice your party manners

One Week Before

collect or buy the game supplies

collect or buy make-and-do supplies

buy or make the favors, prizes, and decorations

check on replies to the invitations

make "take-home" bags for each guest

order any special foods, such as a birthday cake

One Day Before

help your parents clear the party and game area

put up the decorations

get a large carton for garbage

wrap prizes and favors

buy the food (unless you are having it delivered or will eat out)

make special foods that will keep overnight

pick up cake

put the game and make-and-do supplies in a convenient place

On the Day of the Party

Before the Guests Arrive

check what you did yesterday to make sure everything is still in order

make repairs if necessary

clear a space for coats

set out the prizes, favors, and "take-home" bags

put your pets in another room

When the Guests Arrive

greet your guests at the door; accept any presents politely; take coats

direct the guests to the make-and-do table (if you have one)

begin the activities

serve refreshments

give out "take-home" bags, prizes, and favors

say good-by to each guest

After the Guests Have Left

help your parents clean up

play with your presents (if you received any)

think about how much fun you had

Find Out More

If you enjoyed doing the activities in this book, you'll want to check out other arts and crafts resources. Some are listed here. Your school or public library will have many more.

Ages 5–8

Costumes by Clare Beaton (Warwick Press, 1990)
Seventeen different costumes are included in this book. You can make them using old clothing and other things you can find around the house.

Crafts for Kids by Better Homes and Gardens on CD-ROM for Mac (Multicom, 1994)
Fun and simple projects for kids ages 3 to 12. This disc includes instructions for making toys, decorations, snacks, and more.

EcoArt! Earth Friendly Art and Craft Experiences for 3- to 9-year-olds by Laurie Carlson (Williamson Publishing, 1992)
All the projects in this book make use of good ecological practices, like recycling and reusing. You'll learn how to make your own art and craft supplies as well as how to make over ninety different projects.

Face Painting by Jacqueline Russon (Thomson Learning, 1994)
You can turn your face into many different things—from an animal to a season. This book tells you what you need and shows you how to do it.

I Can Make It! Dress Up by Sara Lynn and Diane James (Bantam, 1994)
Bow ties, masks, and badges are just a few of the great things you can make to dress up. Have fun!

I Can Make Puppets by Mary Wallace (Greey de Pencier Books, 1994)
Learn more about how to make pop-up, hand, and finger puppets and how to make a puppet stage.

Make Gifts! by Kim Solga (North Light Books, 1991)
Have fun making these simple gifts, which include trophies and wrapping paper. The materials you'll need are probably already in your home.

The Make-Something-Club: Fun with Crafts, Food, and Gifts by Frances Zweifel (Viking, 1994)
Join Winky, Skipper, and Tag's club and learn how to make pine-cone birdfeeders, pasta necklaces, and paper flowers. You'll also find recipes for making fun snacks.

My First Christmas Activity Book by Angela Wilkes (Dorling Kindersley, 1994)
This book gives you easy instructions for making your own Advent calendar, stockings, tree decorations, and yummy Christmas treats!

My First Music Book by Helen Drew (Dorling Kindersley, 1993)
Start your own band! In this book, you'll learn how to make simple musical instruments from things around the house.

Show-Me-How I Can Make Things: How-to-Make Craft Projects for the Very Young by Sally Walton (Smithmark, 1995)
Jewelry boxes, cork rattlesnakes, monsters, and sock puppets are only a few of the sixteen projects included in this book. The instructions are simple, and the materials can be found in most homes.

Super Toys and Games from Paper by F. Virginia Walter (Sterling Publishing, 1993)
In this book, you'll learn how to make games, toys, and puppets with paper and paper products.

The Way Things Work on CD-ROM for Mac (Dorling Kindersley, 1994)
This CD—for children and adults—is based on David Macaulay's book by the same title. Through animation and sound, over 200 of the author's illustrations come to life.

Ages 9 and Up

Best Ever Paper Airplane Book by Norman Schmidt (Sterling Publishing, 1994)
This book uses simple diagrams and photos to show you how to construct and decorate your own paper airplanes. Eighteen different kinds of planes are included.

Gifts Kids Can Make by Sheila McGraw (Firefly Books, 1994)
Make inexpensive gifts for grandparents, friends, teachers—even your pets! Most materials can be found in your home.

How to Make Super Pop-ups by Joan Irvine (Beech Tree Books, 1992)
All kids love pop-up books and now you can make your own! By following the simple instructions in this book, you can make paper pop-ups of insects, skyscrapers, monsters, and many more things.

The Kids' Multicultural Art Book: Art and Craft Experiences from Around the World by Alexander M. Tergian (Williamson, 1993)
What kinds of arts and crafts do children from Africa or India make? This book tells you and gives you instructions for making them yourself.

Masks by Lyndie Wright (Watts, 1990)
Masks have been around for thousands of years. They've been used by people in all parts of the world for religious and other reasons. This book shows you how to make many different kinds of masks from items found around your home.

Origami: A Children's Book by Irmgard Kneissler (Childrens Press, 1992)
This book shows you how to make all sorts of animals, kites, and boxes out of paper. Make your own puppets and put on a puppet show!

Paper Toys That Fly, Soar, Zoom, and Whistle by E. Richard Churchill (Sterling, 1989)
All you need is paper, tape, and some paper clips to make dozens of toys at home. This book tells you what you need and how to put these toys together.

Paper Tricks and Toys by E. Richard Churchill (Sterling, 1992)
What fun you can have playing tricks on your friends. Just follow the simple instructions in this book and you'll have wonderful toys that will amaze all.

75 Fun Things to Make and Do by Yourself by Karen Gray Ruelle (Sterling, 1993)
Looking for something to do? Make an orchestra out of kazoos, bottle flutes, and glass harmonicas! This how-to book gives instructions for these and seventy-two other projects that you can do all by yourself.

Spring by Ruth Thomson (Watts, 1990)
Spring offers the opportunity to make many things—from dyed eggs to paper flowers.

Woodworking for Kids: 40 Fabulous Fun and Useful Things for Kids to Make by Kevin McGuire (Sterling, 1993)
Learn more about the tools and techniques of beginning woodworking and find instructions for building toys, furniture, animals, gifts, and musical instruments.

Illustration acknowledgments

All photographs in this volume were taken for *Childcraft* by Joseph A. Erhardt unless otherwise noted. All craft items shown in this volume were designed and made by Kathy Belter, Ann Tomasic, Mary Tonon, and Jan Yourist with special assistance from Barbara Lazarus Metz. All diagrams in this volume were prepared by Product Illustration Inc. unless otherwise noted. Page numbers refer to two-page spreads. The words *"(left)," "(center)," "(top)," "(bottom),"* and *"(right)"* indicate position on the spread. All illustrations are the exclusive property of the publishers of *Childcraft*.

1:	art, Lynne Cherry
6-7:	Marshall Berman
8-33:	Lynne Cherry
34-35:	Marshall Berman
36-37:	Diagrams *(center left and bottom right)* by Bill and Judie Anderson
40-41:	Ellen Raskin
44-45:	Linda Gist
46-47:	Trina Schart Hyman
56-57:	Trina Schart Hyman
58-59:	Linda Gist
66-67:	Diagram *(top left)* by Bill and Judie Anderson
68-69:	Ellen Raskin
70-71:	Trina Schart Hyman
72-73:	Stephen Hale; Ellen Raskin
78-79:	Stephen Hale
82-83:	Ellen Raskin
88-89:	Diagram *(left)* by Bill and Judie Anderson
90-91:	Linda Gist
92-93:	Ellen Raskin
94-95:	Trina Schart Hyman
108-109:	Diagram *(left)* by Bill and Judie Anderson
112-113:	Angela Adams
118-121:	Trina Schart Hyman
126-127:	Linda Gist
136-137:	Angela Adams
140-149:	Linda Gist
154-155:	Diagram *(center right)* by Bill and Judie Anderson
160-161:	Trina Schart Hyman
166-167:	Linda Gist
170-171:	Ellen Raskin
172-173:	Photos *(left and center right)* by Jan Yourist
188-189:	Linda Gist
202-203:	Diagram *(center left)* by Bill and Judie Anderson
208-209:	Stephen Hale
210-211:	Trina Schart Hyman
212-243:	Angela Adams
246-255:	Dora Leder
262-267:	Trina Schart Hyman
268-270:	Bill and Judie Anderson
274-290:	Trina Schart Hyman
294-295:	Trina Schart Hyman; diagram by Bill and Judie Anderson
298-311:	Linda Gist
Cover:	Roberta Polfus

Index

This index is an alphabetical list of the important topics covered in this book. It will help you find information given in both words *and* pictures. To help you understand what an entry means, there is often a helping word in parentheses, for example, **Dog and Bone** (game). If there is information in both words and pictures, you will see the words *(with pictures)* after the page number. If there is *only* a picture, you will see the word *(picture)* after the page number. If you do not find what you want in this index, please go to the General Index in Volume 15, which is a key to all of the books.